Study Guide to Accompany

Computers and Data Processing
CONCEPTS AND APPLICATIONS

Third Edition

WITH BASIC

Steven L. Mandell
Bowling Green State University

West Publishing Company
St. Paul   New York   Los Angeles   San Francisco

COPYRIGHT © 1985 by WEST PUBLISHING CO.
50 West Kellogg Boulevard
P.O. Box 43526
St. Paul, MN 55164

ISBN   0-314-87130-6

CONTENTS

iii

BASIC SUPPLEMENT

INTRODUCTION

This study guide has been designed to accompany **Computers and Data Processing: Concepts and Applications**, 3rd edition published by West Publishing Company. Throughout its development, emphasis has been placed on providing a vehicle that can assist the student in learning the text material. No design will ever take the place of conscientious student effort; however, the approaches incorporated within this study guide will make the task less difficult.

The structure of the study guide parallels the textbook. Within each chapter the student will encounter distinct segments. A list of KEY TERMS with definitions is provided at the beginning to orient the student toward the important concepts covered in the text. Following the key terms is a CHAPTER SUMMARY. A series of multiple choice questions with explanatory answers has been formatted into a STRUCTURED LEARNING environment. Utilizing this technique, the student can "walk through" the material in a progressive fashion. TRUE/FALSE and MATCHING questions permit the student to obtain immediate feedback on comprehension. SHORT ANSWER exercises provide the student with an opportunity to express an understanding of the material. Solutions to the odd-numbered problems are presented in an ANSWER KEY so that the student can evaluate and diagnose progress.

The supplement to the study guide is designed to support the BASIC programming supplement found in an optional version of the text. The section structure also parallels the text material; however, a slightly different format is utilized. A scaled-down version of STRUCTURED LEARNING is presented initially as a review mechanism. A WORKSHEET is then provided for the student to apply programming concepts and techniques. Two PROGRAMMING PROBLEMS are presented as the ultimate evaluation exercise for each section. Once again the solution for the odd numbered problem is incorporated into an ANSWER KEY.

Good luck!

Steven L. Mandell

1

Introduction to Data Processing

KEY TERMS

Accuracy – The constancy of computer-generated results.

Automatic data processing (ADP) – The collection, manipulation, and dissemination of data by electromechanical machines to attain specified objectives.

Calculate – To perform arithmetic and/or logical manipulations of data.

Classify – To categorize data according to certain characteristics so that they are meaningful to the user.

Code – To convert data into a form that the computer can read.

Collect – To gather data from various sources and assemble them at one location.

Communicate – A step in the output phase of data flow; to transfer information in intelligible form to a user.

Computer – A general-purpose machine with applications limited only by the creativity of the humans who use it; its power is derived from its speed, accuracy, and memory.

Computer-assisted instruction (CAI) – Direct interaction between a computer and a student in which the computer serves as an instructor.

Convert – To translate information into a form people can read.

Data – Facts; the raw material of information.

Data base – The cornerstone of a management information system; basic data are commonly defined and consistently organized to fit the information needs of a wide variety of users in an organization.

Data processing – A systematic set of techniques for collecting, manipulating, and disseminating data to achieve specified objectives.

Dedicated machine – A computer that has been specifically adapted to perform specific tasks.

Electronic data processing (EDP) – Data processing performed largely by electronic equipment, such as computers, rather than by manual or mechanical methods.

Field – A meaningful item of data, such as a social security number.

File – A grouping of related records; sometimes referred to as a data set.

Garbage in-garbage out (GIGO) – A phrase used to exemplify the fact that the meaningfulness of data-processing results relies on the accuracy or relevancy of the data fed into the processor.

General-purpose machine – Computers that can be used for a variety of purposes.

Information – Data that have been organized and processed so that they are meaningful.

Input – Data that are submitted to the computer for processing.

Instruction set – The fundamental logical and arithmetic procedures that the computer can perform, such as addition, subtraction, and comparison.

Memory – The part of the computer that provides the ability to recall information.

Output – Information that comes from the computer as a result of processing.

Primary memory – Also known as internal storage, memory, main storage; the section of the CPU that holds instructions, data and intermediate and final results during processing.

Record – A collection of data items, or fields, that relates to a single unit.

Retrieve – The accessing of previously stored information by the computer so that it can be referenced by the user.

Secondary storage – Also known as external or auxiliary storage; supplements primary storage but operates at a slower speed.

Sort – To arrange data elements into a predetermined sequence to facilitate processing.

Special-purpose machine – See Dedicated machine.

Store – To retain processed data for future reference.

Summarize – To reduce large amounts of data to a more concise and usable form.

Verify – To check the accuracy and completeness of data.

Word processor – An application software package that performs text-editing functions.

SUMMARY

Computers have no intelligence. They perform tasks that have been predetermined by human beings. The three basic functions that computers can perform are arithmetic operations, comparison operations, and storage and retrieval operations. To perform these operations, computers follow an instruction set that is built into the computer's circuitry.

General-purpose computers can be used for many applications. Special-purpose or dedicated machines perform specialized tasks.

Computers derive most of their power from their speed, accuracy, and memory. Speed is determined by the switching speed of circuits and the distances electric currents have to travel.   Computer speed is expressed as the time required to perform one operation.

Computer accuracy refers to internal operations.   The electronic circuitry of a computer performs the same way each time a computer is used.   If inaccurate information is input into a computer, then the output will be inaccurate.   This is the garbage in-garbage out (GIGO) concept.

Memory is the part of a computer that stores data.   Primary memory is located inside the computer.   Secondary storage is located on external storage devices.   Secondary storage holds data not immediately needed by the computer.

Collecting, manipulating, and distributing data is known as data processing.   The term automatic data processing (ADP) describes early electromechanical devices used to process data. Manipulating data with a computer is known as electronic data processing (EDP).   The objective of data processing is to con-vert raw data into information that can be used in decision making.

All data processing follows the same basic flow: input, processing, output.   The input operation involves three steps: collecting, verifying, and coding.   This is followed by five processing steps: classifying, sorting, calculating, sum-marizing, and storing.   The output phase of data flow involves retrieving, converting, and communicating the information.

Data must be organized to be processed effectively.   The smallest unit of data is called a field.   A group of related fields is called a record.   A grouping of related records is a file, and a collection of files is a data base.

We are in the midst of a computer revolution.   The com-puter's low cost and expanded capabilities have contributed to advances in many areas of our lives.   In business, word proc-essing is just one application where computers have simplified tedious jobs.   In education, computer-assisted instruction (CAI) involves interaction between a computer and a student.   The impact of computers on society is growing as we become increasingly dependent upon computers in our daily lives.

STRUCTURED LEARNING

1. A computer can perform all of the following except
    a. adding, subtracting, multiplying, and dividing
    b. exercising independent intelligence to solve problems
    c. storing and retrieving information
    d. comparing numeric and alphabetic characters

    *   *   *   *   *   *   *   *   *

    (b) A computer can perform only the instructions supplied
    by a human being; it cannot perform any tasks that a person
    has not predetermined.

2. A computer that can be used for many purposes is referred
    to as a
    a. dedicated machine   c. general-purpose machine
    b. special-purpose machine   d. all of the above

    *   *   *   *   *   *   *   *   *

    (c) Special-purpose or dedicated computers are similar to
    general-purpose computers, but they have been adapted to
    perform specialized tasks.

3. Computers derive most of their power from
    a. speed   c. memory
    b. accuracy   d. all of the above

    *   *   *   *   *   *   *   *   *

    (d) The speed and accuracy of computer operations and the
    virtually unlimited recall of data make the computer a
    powerful and effective tool.

4. The accuracy of a computer relates to its
    a. internal operations   c. input
    b. external operations   d. secondary storage

    *   *   *   *   *   *   *   *   *

    (a) Computer accuracy is largely due to the reliability of
    the electronic circuits that make up a computer. Accuracy
    does not refer to the data that is put into a computer. If
    inaccurate data is put into a computer, then the output
    will be inaccurate.

5.   The flow pattern for data processing is
      a.   processing, input, output
      b.   processing, output, input
      c.   output, input, processing
      d.   input, processing, output

      *   *   *   *   *   *   *   *   *

      (d) To derive information from data, all data processing
      follows the same basic pattern of input, processing, out-
      put.

6.   Inputting data involves three steps:
      a.   collecting, calculating, and classifying
      b.   collecting, verifying, and coding
      c.   calculating, classifying, and coding
      d.   sorting, summarizing, and storing

      *   *   *   *   *   *   *   *   *

      (b) Data must be gathered from various sources (collected)
      and assembled at one location where its accuracy and
      completeness are then checked (verified). The data must
      then be converted into a form that the computer can read
      (coded).

7.   Which of the following is not a step involved in processing
      data?
      a.   verifying   c.   sorting
      b.   classifying   d.   calculating

      *   *   *   *   *   *   *   *   *

      (a) Verifying data should be a part of inputting. The
      processing stage of data processing can involve classi-
      fying, sorting, calculating, summarizing, and storing.

8.   Which of the following represents the arrangement of data
      items from the most simple element to the most complex?
      a.   field, file, record, data base
      b.   field, record, file, data base
      c.   file, field, record, data base
      d.   data base, record, field, file

      *   *   *   *   *   *   *   *   *

      (b) Data should be organized in a way that is useful to the
      user. The careful structuring of data elements leads to
      efficient processing and effective decision making.

9.   A file is
     a.   a single meaningful item of data
     b.   a collection of related fields that relate to a single
          unit
     c.   a grouping of related records
     d.   data that have been organized and processed in a
          meaningful way

     *   *   *   *   *   *   *   *   *

     (c) Records pertaining to a common application form a file.
     For example, all the information about a single employee
     might form a file.

10. Which of the following is not true of computers?
     a.   They are increasing their impact on our daily lives.
     b.   They are well suited for applications that are well
          defined, repetitive, and involve a large number of
          records.
     c.   They are much like any other tool used by humans: they
          increase problem-solving capabilities and the capacity
          to handle complex relationships.
     d.   Their impact on our daily lives is decreasing as their
          cost and size decrease.

     *   *   *   *   *   *   *   *   *

     (d) Computers are increasing in use in society and their
     impact is felt in almost every area of our lives.

TRUE/FALSE

1.   T   F   The success of the computer can be directly attrib-
             uted to the imagination of people.

2.   T   F   The number of unique instructions required to direct
             a computer's functions is often less than a hundred.

3.   T   F   Primary memory is also referred to as external
             storage.

4.   T   F   Automatic data processing describes the use of
             electronic computers to collect, distribute, and
             manipulate data.

5.   T   F   Collect, classify, sort, and summarize are terms used
             to refer to the input phase of data processing.

6.   T   F   Retrieve, convert, and communicate are the three
              steps involved in the output phase of data flow.

7.   T   F   To achieve effective data processing, data needs to
              be organized before the processing stage.

8.   T   F   Data that have been organized and processed are
              called raw facts.

9.   T   F   A dedicated machine can be used for many purposes.

10.   T   F   Computer-assisted instruction is possible through
              direct interaction between the computer and the stu-
              dent.

MATCHING

a. memory   f. input, processing, output
b. data   g. dedicated
c. garbage in-garbage out   h. computer-assisted
d. record   instruction
e. output   i. accuracy
                                    j. general-purpose

1.   The reliability of the electronic circuits that are inside
      a computer is referred to as a computer's _____.

2.   Incorrect input used by a computer results in incorrect
      output. This concept is known as _____.

3.   The part of a computer where data are stored is the com-
      puter's _____.

4.   Raw facts that have been collected from different sources
      but do not allow meaningful conclusions without some proc-
      essing are _____.

5.   A collection of individual data items that relate to a
      single unit is called a(n) _____.

6.   The basic pattern of all data processing is _____.

7.   A computer that is designed to perform a specific task is
      referred to as a(n) _____ machine.

8.   Since most computers can be used for many purposes, they
     are referred to as _____ machines.

9.   Information generated by a computer as a result of proc-
     essing is called _____.

10. An educational application that involves direct interaction
     between a computer and a student is called _____.

SHORT ANSWER

1.   What are the three basic functions a computer can perform?

2.   What two factors control the speed of a computer?

3.   Into what two parts is a computer's memory divided?

4.   What is the objective of all data processing, whether manual, electromechanical, or electronic?

5.   What is the difference between data and information?

6.   What is the flow pattern in all data processing?

7.   Describe the steps involved in the first phase of data processing.

8. Briefly describe the steps involved in the last phase of data processing.

9. How should data be organized?

10. Why are some people concerned about the increased use of computers?

ANSWER KEY

True/False

1. T   3. F   5. F   7. T   9. F

Matching

1. i   3. a   5. d   7. g   9. e

Short Answer

1. ● add, subtract, multiply, and divide
    ● compare
    ● store and retrieve information

3. A computer's memory is divided into primary memory and secondary storage.

5. Data refer to raw facts that have been collected from various sources but which are not in a useful form for decision making. Information is data that have been organized and processed. This makes it valuable for decision-making purposes.

7. Collecting involves gathering data from various sources and assembling them in one location. Verifying involves checking the data for accuracy and completeness. Coding involves converting the data into machine-readable form.

9. They should be organized in a way so that anticipated needs of users for information can be met.

The Evolution
of Computers

KEY TERMS

Accounting machine - Forerunner of the computer; could mechanically read data from punched cards, perform calculations, rearrange data, and print results in varied formats.

Analytical engine - A machine created by Charles Babbage, capable of addition, subtraction, multiplication, division, and storage of intermediate results in a memory unit; too advanced for its time, the analytical engine was forgotten for nearly one hundred years.

Application-oriented language - A language that focuses on the computational and logical procedures required to solve a problem.

Architecture - Another name for the internal design of a computer.

Atanasoff-Berry Computer (ABC) - Determined to be the first electronic computer; developed by John Vincent Atanasoff and Clifford Berry.

Batch processing - The grouping of user jobs for processing one after another in a continuous stream--a batch processing environment.

COBOL (COmmon Business-Oriented Language) - A high-level programming language generally used for accounting and business data processing.

Difference engine – A machine developed by Charles Babbage in 1822; used to compute mathematical tables with results up to five significant digits in length.

Direct access – Also random-access processing; a method of processing in which data is submitted to the computer as it occurs; individual records can be located and updated without reading all preceding files.

EDSAC (Electronic Display Storage Automatic Computer) – The first stored-program computer.

EDVAC (Electronic Discrete Variable Automatic Computer) – A stored-program computer developed at the University of Pennsylvania.

ENIAC (Electronic Numerical Integrator And Calculator) – Developed by J. Presper Eckert and John W. Mauchly at the University of Pennsylvania.

First-generation computers – Used vacuum tubes; developed in the 1950s; much faster than earlier mechanical devices, but very slow in comparison to today's computers.

FORTRAN (FORmula TRANslator) – A programming language used primarily in performing mathematical or scientific operations.

Fourth-generation computers – Use large-scale integration and offer significant price and performance improvements over earlier computers.

Hardware – The physical components that make up a computer system.

High-level languages – English-like coding schemes that are procedure-, problem-, and user-oriented.

Hollerith code – An 80-column punched card.

Integrated circuits (ICs) – Small chips less than 1/8-inch square containing hundreds of electronic components permitting much faster processing at a greatly reduced price.

Large-scale integration (LSI) circuits – Circuits containing thousands of transistors densely packed on a single silicon chip.

Machine language – The only set of instructions that a computer can execute directly; a code that designates the proper electrical states in the computer as combinations of 0s and 1s.

Machine-oriented language – A language which describes program functions and execution; very similar to actual machine language.

Magnetic core – An iron-alloy, doughnut-shaped ring about the size of a pinhead of which memory can be composed; an individual core can store one binary digit (its state is determined by the direction of an electrical current).

Magnetic disk – A storage medium consisting of a metal platter coated on both sides with a magnetic recording material upon which data is stored in the form of magnetized spots.

Magnetic drum – A cylinder with a magnetic outer surface on which data are stored.

Magnetic tape – A storage medium consisting of a narrow strip upon which spots of iron-oxide are magnetized to represent data; a sequential storage medium.

Mainframe – See Central processing unit.

Mark I – The first automatic calculator.

Microcomputer – A computer small in size but not in power; now available in 8-, 16-, 32-bit microprocessor configurations.

Microprocessor – The CPU of a microcomputer.

Minicomputer – A computer with the components of a full-sized system but having a smaller primary storage capacity.

Mnemonics – A symbolic name (memory aid); used in symbolic languages (for example, assembly language) and high-level programming languages.

Online – In direct communication with the computer.

Operating system – A collection of programs designed to permit a computer system to manage itself and to avoid idle CPU time while increasing utilization of computer resources.

Primary memory – Also known as internal storage, memory, main storage; the section of the CPU that holds instructions, data, and intermediate and final results during processing.

Problem-oriented language – A language which describes the problem and solution without detailing the computational procedures.

Punched card – An outdated form of sequential storage in which the data is represented by the presence or absence of strategically placed holes.

Read/write head – An electromagnet used as a component of a tape or disk drive; in reading, it detects magnetized areas and translates them into electrical pulses; in writing, it magnetizes appropriate areas, thereby erasing data stored previously.

Remote terminal – A terminal that is placed at a location distant from the central computer.

Secondary storage – Also known as external or auxiliary storage; supplements primary storage but operates at a slower speed.

Second-generation computers – 1959-1964; used magnetic cores for primary storage; magnetic tapes for secondary storage; first use of high-level programming languages.

Software – Programs used to direct the computer for problem solving and overseeing operations.

Software package – A set of standardized computer programs, procedures, and related documentation designed to solve problems of a specific application; often acquired from an external supplier.

Stored-program computer – A computer that stores instructions for operations to be performed in electronic form, in primary storage.

Symbolic language – Also known as assembly language; uses mnemonic symbols to represent instructions; must be translated to machine language before it can be executed by the computer.

Third-generation computers – 1965-1970; characterized by the use of integrated circuits, reduced size, lower costs, and increased speed and reliability.

Time-sharing – An arrangement in which two or more users can access the same central computer system and receive what seem to be simultaneous results.

Transistor – A type of circuitry characteristic of second-generation computers; smaller, faster, and more reliable than vacuum tubes but inferior to third-generation, large-scale integration.

UNIVAC I (UNIVersal Automatic Computer) – One of the first commercial electronic computers; became available in 1951.

User friendly – An easy-to-use, understandable software design that makes it easy for non-computer personnel to use an application software package.

Very large-scale integration (VLSI) – Use of large-scale integration to offer significant price and performance improvements over earlier computers.

SUMMARY

Many different inventions from a variety of fields have had an impact upon the development of computers. Shepherds used knots tied in string to count their herds. Manual calculating devices such as the abacus, Napier's Bones, and the slide rule were forerunners of the modern computer.

The development of the first mechanical calculator is attributed to Blaise Pascal, about the year 1642. Pascal's calculator added and subtracted numbers by using a series of rotating gears. Gottfried von Leibnitz developed a machine that could add, subtract, multiply, divide, and calculate square roots. His machine also used rotating gears.

Punched cards were first used by Joseph Jacquard, a weaver. Jacquard used punched cards to control the patterns that were woven on his loom. The concept of using punched cards as a means of supplying instructions to a machine is still in use today. Charles Babbage used punched cards in a calculating machine. His difference and analytical engines were too advanced for the technology of the 1830s, but his work earned him the title "father of computers."

In the late 1880s, Herman Hollerith developed what we know as the standard 12-row by 80-column punched card. Hollerith also developed a coding scheme, known as the Hollerith Code, that was used to process census data for the United States government. The Tabulating Machine Company, started by Hollerith, merged with other companies and became IBM.

During the 1930s and 1940s, several devices were created that contributed to the development of the modern-day computer. The ABC was a working model of a serial, binary, electromechanical computer. The Mark I was an electromagnetic device. ENIAC was an electronic computer and EDVAC and EDSAC used the stored-program concept.

UNIVAC I was the first commercial electronic computer, and it marked the beginning of first-generation computers. First-generation computers were very large, hot, and unreliable. They used vacuum tubes and magnetic drum memory.

Second-generation computers were smaller, faster, and more reliable. Transistors replaced vacuum tubes and magnetic cores replaced magnetic drums. During the second generation, advances were made in the areas of secondary storage, high-level languages, and processing modes.

Integrated circuits reduced the size and increased the speed of third-generation computers. Minicomputers were developed during this period, bringing computing power to many businesses for the first time. Software development became a separate industry due to the growing need for reliable software.

Fourth-generation computers were characterized by large-scale integration (LSI) and very large-scale integration (VLSI). The fourth generation has continued the pattern established in other generations. That pattern is reduced size of computers and increased speed and accuracy. During the fourth generation the concept of user friendly computers developed.

Mainframe computers are the oldest type of computers. They were expensive and dominated the industry until the development of minicomputers. Minicomputers are more flexible than mainframes, and they are used in many businesses. The success of microcomputers can be attributed to a few people with ingenious ideas in product development and marketing.

STRUCTURED LEARNING

1. The analytical engine, a forerunner of the modern computer, was developed by
    a. Pascal   c. Babbage
    b. Leibnitz   d. Hollerith

    *   *   *   *   *   *   *   *   *

(c) The analytical engine designed by Babbage was too advanced for its time. It was not until nearly 100 years later that Babbage's concepts and ideas were implemented.

2. The concept of using punched cards to give instructions to a machine was first used by
    a. Hollerith
    b. Jacquard
    c. Babbage
    d. von Leibnitz

    *   *   *   *   *   *   *   *   *

(b) Jacquard used punched cards during the early 1800s to control the patterns that were woven with his loom. In the late 1800s, Hollerith used punched cards to complete the census.

3. The first automatic calculator developed by Aiken at Harvard University was
    a. ENIAC
    b. EDSAC
    c. EDVAC
    d. Mark I

    *   *   *   *   *   *   *   *   *

(d) The Mark I used electromagnetic relays that produced a loud clicking sound. ENIAC, EDSAC, and EDVAC were all developed after the Mark I computer.

4. The first stored-program computers were
    a. EDSAC and EDVAC
    b. ENIAC and EDVAC
    c. ABC and Mark I
    d. ENIAC and Mark I

    *   *   *   *   *   *   *   *   *

(a) Two groups of people were working on the stored-program concept at the same time. In the United States, the University of Pennsylvania sponsored a group that developed EDVAC. In England, a group at Cambridge University created EDSAC.

5. First-generation computers were characterized by the use of
    a. magnetic disks
    b. magnetic tape
    c. vacuum tubes
    d. VLSI

    *   *   *   *   *   *   *   *   *

(c) Vacuum tubes used in first-generation computers generated heat and were very slow in processing. The computers were huge and required special air conditioning equipment to dissipate the heat from the vacuum tubes.

6. What replaced magnetic drums as a storage medium in second-generation computers?
    a. magnetic disks   c. paper tape
    b. punched cards   d. magnetic cores

    *   *   *   *   *   *   *   *   *

    (d) Magnetic cores replaced magnetic drums as the primary internal storage medium. Paper tape and punched cards are representative of first-generation computers. Magnetic disks are associated with third- and fourth-generation machines.

7. Third-generation computers introduced
    a. magnetic cores as the primary internal storage medium
    b. the use of vacuum tubes in electronic circuits
    c. extensive use of high-level programming languages
    d. microprocessors and microcomputers

    *   *   *   *   *   *   *   *   *

    (c) Many high-level languages were developed during the second generation of computers, but they were used extensively in third-generation computers.

8. The emphasis on ease of use and application in fourth-generation computers is referred to as
    a. user friendly   c. user easy
    b. user compatible   d. user understood

    *   *   *   *   *   *   *   *   *

    (a) As computers have become smaller and faster, their use has increased. More and more people without technical backgrounds are using computers, so they have become more user friendly.

9. Languages such as FORTRAN and COBOL are examples of
    a. machine language   c. symbolic language
    b. high-level language   d. mnemonics

    *   *   *   *   *   *   *   *   *

    (b) FORTRAN and COBOL are high-level languages. They are easily readable by humans but cannot be directly executed by the computer.

10.   One reason for the continued popularity of minicomputers is
      a.   economies of scale   c.   flexibility
      b.   low capital investment   d.   availability of software

*   *   *   *   *   *   *   *   *

(c) Minicomputers can be plugged into standard electrical
outlets; they do not require special facilities; they can
be utilized in an unlimited number of configurations.

TRUE/FALSE

1.   T   F   Herman Hollerith founded a company that later became
             IBM.

2.   T   F   The analytical engine, an automatic mechanical cal-
             culator, was built by Charles Babbage.

3.   T   F   In the late 1800s Herman Hollerith was commissioned
             by the United States government to reduce the time
             required to process the census data.

4.   T   F   Punched cards were first used by Joseph Jacquard.

5.   T   F   The ABC was developed by Eckert and Mauchly at the
             University of Pennsylvania.

6.   T   F   The Mark I was the first commercial computer, and
             its creation marked the beginning of the first
             generation of computers.

7   T   F   Symbolic languages were first developed during the
             second generation of computers.

8.   T   F   Magnetic tapes increased processing speeds in
             second-generation computers.

9.   T   F   The software development industry emerged during the
             fourth generation of computers.

10. T   F   Magnetic core storage is a characteristic of
             fourth-generation computers.

MATCHING

a. Atanasoff   f. Hollerith
b. von Neumann   g. Pascal
c. Babbage   h. Mauchly and Eckert
d. magnetic cores   i. Jacquard
e. transistors   j. microcomputer

1. Punched cards were developed as a means of controlling a loom by _____.

2. Machines used in processing the 1890 census were developed by _____.

3. Vacuum tubes were replaced by _____ in second-generation computers.

4. The stored-program concept was based on principles developed by _____.

5. ENIAC and UNIVAC I were both developed by _____.

6. The first mechanical calculator invented by _____ could only add and subtract.

7. A microprocessor, together with other densely packed chips for storage and input/output operations, form a _____.

8. _____ was responsible for both the analytical and difference engines.

9. _____ replaced magnetic drums as the primary internal storage medium in second-generation computers.

10. Clifford Berry worked with _____ to develop the ABC computer.

SHORT ANSWER

1.   Why did many of the programs written for second-generation computers have to be rewritten for third-generation computers?

2.   How did the software industry begin?

3.   What are the characteristics of first-generation computers?

4.   What are the characteristics of second-generation computers?

5.   What are the characteristics of third-generation computers?

6.   What are the characteristics of fourth-generation computers?

7.   What distinguished EDSAC and EDVAC from previous computers?

8.   What are some of the reasons minicomputers have remained popular?

9. What are the names of some of the people who contributed to the growth of microcomputers and with what companies are they associated?

10. What are a few of the major drawbacks associated with first-generation computers that severely restricted their applicability?

ANSWER KEY

True/False

1. T   3. T   5. F   7. F   9. F

Matching

1. i   3. e   5. h   7. j   9. d

Short Answer

1. Programs written for second-generation computers were based on an architecture or internal design different from the internal architecture of third-generation computers. Therefore, the programs had to be rewritten to fit the new architecture.

3.   ● vacuum tubes
      ● magnetic drum memory
      ● large size
      ● heat
      ● unreliability

5.   ● use of integrated circuits
      ● extensive use of high-level programming languages
      ● emergence of minicomputers
      ● remote processing and time sharing

7.   They used the stored-program concept. This feature allowed
      the computers to run without human intervention.

9.   ● Charles Tandy--Radio Shack
      ● Jack Tramiel--Commodore Business Machines
      ● Steven Jobs and Stephen Wozniak--Apple Computers
      ● Adam Osborne--Osborne Computer Corporation

Hardware

KEY TERMS

Address – A unique identifier assigned to each memory location within primary storage.

American Standard Code for Information Interchange (ASCII) – A seven-bit standard code used for information interchange among data-processing systems, communication systems, and associated equipment.

Analog computer – A computer that measures continuous electrical or physical magnitudes rather than operating on digits; contrast with digital computer.

Arithmetic/logic unit (ALU) – The section of the CPU that handles arithmetic computations and logical operations.

ASCII-8 – An eight-bit version of ASCII.

Auxiliary storage – See Secondary storage.

Base 2 – See Binary number system.

Base 8 – See Octal number system.

Base 16 – See Hexadecimal number system.

Binary number system – The numeric system used in computer operations that uses the digits 0 and 1 and has a base of 2.

Binary representation – Uses a two-state, or binary, system to represent data; as in setting and resetting the electrical state of semiconductor memory to either 0 or 1.

Binary system – See Binary number system.

Biochip – A primary memory chip that uses the grouping of molecules to create an electronic circuit; none have actually been made.

Bit (short for BInary digiT) – The smallest unit of information that can be represented in binary notation.

Bit cells – The name for storage locations in semiconductors.

Bubble memory – A memory device in which data is represented by magnetized spots (magnetic domains) that rest on a thin film of semiconductor material.

Byte – A fixed number of adjacent bits operated on as a unit.

Cache memory – Also known as a high-speed buffer; a working buffer or temporary area used to help speed the execution of a program.

Capacitor – The device that holds the electrical charge within a bit cell of semiconductor memory.

Central processing unit (CPU) – Also known as the mainframe or heart of the computer; composed of three sections--the primary storage unit, arithmetic/logic unit (ALU), and control unit.

Check bit – See Parity bit.

Control unit – The section of the CPU that directs the sequence of operations by electrical signals and governs the actions of the various units which make up the computer.

Decimal number system – A number system based on the powers of ten.

Digital computer – The type of computer commonly used in business applications; operates on distinct data (for example, digits) by performing arithmetic and logic processes on specific data units.

Dump - A hard-copy printout of the contents of computer memory; valuable in debugging programs.

Erasable programmable read-only memory (EPROM) - This memory unit can be erased and reprogrammed, but only by being submitted to a special process.

Even parity - A method of coding in which an even number of 1 bits represent each character; used to enhance the detection of errors.

Extended Binary Coded Decimal Interchange Code (EBCDIC) - An 8-bit code for character representation.

External storage - See Secondary storage.

Four-bit Binary Coded Decimal (BCD) - A four-bit binary digit computer code that uses the unique combinations of zone bits and numeric bits to represent specific characters.

Hard-wired - Memory instructions that cannot be changed or deleted by other stored-program instructions.

Hexadecimal number system - A base 16 number system commonly used when printing the contents of primary storage to aid programmers in detecting errors.

Internal storage - See Primary storage.

K - A symbol used to denote 1024 (2^{10}) storage units when referring to a computer's primary storage capacity.

Magnetic domain - A magnetized spot representing data in bubble memory.

Mainframe - See Central processing unit.

Main storage - See Primary storage.

Maxicomputers - See Supercomputers.

Microprogram - A sequence of instructions wired into read-only memory; used to tailor a system to meet the user's processing requirements.

Next-sequential-instruction feature - The ability of a computer to execute program steps in the order in which they are stored in memory unless branching takes place.

Nondestructive read/destructive write – The feature of computer memory that permits data to be read and retained in its original state, allowing it to be referenced repeatedly during processing.

Numeric bits – The four right-most bit positions of 6-bit BCD used to encode numeric data.

Octal number system – Each position represents a power of eight.

Odd parity – A method of coding in which an odd number of 1 bits is used to represent each character; facilitates error checking.

Operand – The part of an instruction that tells where to find the data or equipment to be operated on.

Operation code – Also known as op code; the part of an instruction that tells what operation is to be performed.

Parity bit – A means of detecting erroneous transmission of data; internal self-checking to determine if the number of 1 bits in a bit pattern is either odd or even.

Primary memory – See Primary storage.

Primary storage – Also known as internal storage, primary memory, main storage; the section of the CPU that holds instructions, data, and intermediate and final results during processing.

Program – A series of step-by-step instructions that provides a problem solution and tells the computer exactly what to do; of two types--application and system.

Programmable read-only memory (PROM) – Read-only memory that can be programmed by the manufacturer or by the user for special functions to meet the unique needs of the user.

Programmer – The person who writes step-by-step instructions for the computer to execute.

ROM (read-only memory) – The part of computer hardware containing items that cannot be deleted or changed by stored-program instructions because they are wired into the computer.

Register – An internal computer component used for temporary storage of an instruction or data; capable of accepting, holding, and transferring that instruction or data very rapidly.

Secondary storage – Also known as external or auxiliary storage; supplements primary storage but operates at slower speeds.

Semiconductor memory – Circuitry on silicon chips that are smaller than magnetic cores and allow for faster processing; more expensive than core memory and requires a constant power source.

Silicon chip – Solid-logic circuitry used in primary storage units of third- and fourth-generation computers.

Six-bit binary coded decimal – A data representation scheme that is used to represent the decimal digits 0 through 9, the letters A through Z, and 28 special characters.

Stored program – Instructions stored in the computer's memory in electronic form; can be executed repeatedly during processing.

Stored-program concept – The idea that program instructions can be stored in primary storage in electronic form so that no human intervention is required; allows computer to process the instructions at its own speed.

Supercomputers – Large, sophisticated computers that are capable of performing millions of calculations per second and processing enormous amounts of data.

Transistor – A type of circuitry characteristic of second-generation computers; smaller, faster, and more reliable than vacuum tubes but inferior to third-generation, large-scale integration.

Variables – Meaningful names assigned by the programmer to storage locations.

Word – A memory location within primary storage; varies in size (number of bits) from computer to computer.

Zone bit – Used in different combinations with numeric bits to represent numbers, letters, and special characters.

SUMMARY

The central processing unit is the heart of any computer. It is composed of three units: the control unit, the arithmetic/logic unit (ALU), and primary storage. The control unit directs the operations of the computer. The ALU makes calculations and comparisons. Primary storage holds results, data, and programs.

While operating, the control unit decodes a series of instructions. Each instruction contains an op code which indicates the operation to be performed and an operand which gives the storage location of the data to be used. Since the computer operates on instructions sequentially, instructions are placed in consecutive locations in memory. This is known as the next-sequential-instruction feature.

A program is a series of instructions that tell the computer the operation that is to be performed. When programs are placed in primary storage they become stored programs. Once instructions and data are placed in memory, they can be read over and over. The instructions will not be erased until the computer writes over the storage location. This is known as nondestructive read/destructive write.

To direct processing operations, the control unit of the CPU must be able to locate each instruction and data item in storage. Each storage location is assigned an address. The names assigned to storage locations are called variables. They are called variables because the data stored at the location can change.

Primary storage consists of all storage that is part of the CPU. It may be supplemented by secondary storage which is separate from the CPU. Secondary storage is also called auxiliary or external storage. Magnetic tape and magnetic disk are the most common types of secondary storage.

Semiconductors store data in locations called bit cells. The data is represented by "on" or "off" states of electricity. Semiconductor memory requires a constant power source since data is represented by electrical currents. Bubble memory consists of magnetized spots on a film of semiconductor material. Bubble memory does not require a constant power source.

When functions are built into the hardware of a computer, they are placed in read-only memory (ROM). ROM cannot be changed or deleted by stored-program instructions. Programmable read-only memory (PROM) can be programmed only once. Erasable programmable read-only memory can be erased, but only by a special process.

Registers are temporary holding areas for data located in the CPU, but they are not part of primary storage. Cache memory is a portion of primary storage used to help speed the processing operations of the computer. Cache memory serves as a temporary area to store instructions and data that must be accessed a great deal by the program being executed.

Data are stored by the computer as the presence or absence of electricity. These states are represented by zeros and ones. This is called binary representation, and it is planned on the base-2 number system. Many computers today use the octal (base-8) or hexadecimal (base-16) number systems.

Some computers use coding schemes to represent numbers. Some of the most popular are 4-bit and 6-bit binary coded decimal. These coding schemes use a set of 4 bits to represent each digit of a number. Additional bits are used to represent letters. EBCDIC and ASCII-8 use eight bits.

Most computers have a parity or check bit that ensures that data are stored correctly. A parity bit may be either even or odd.

Computers are usually classified as either digital or analog. Digital computers operate on discrete "on" or "off" signals. Analog computers measure continuous physical or electrical changes. Analog computers obtain their results indirectly and are less accurate than digital computers.

Current technology has made it difficult to distinguish between mainframe computers, minicomputers, and microcomputers. Supercomputers or maxicomputers were developed to meet the need for higher processing speeds and greater efficiency.

STRUCTURED LEARNING

1.   Which of the following is not a part of the central processing unit?
     a.   control unit   c.   arithmetic/logic unit
     b.   core unit   d.   primary storage

        *   *   *   *   *   *   *   *   *

(b) The CPU is composed of the control unit, the arithmetic/logic unit and the primary storage unit.

2. What are the functions of the control unit?
    a. directs the sequence of operations
    b. interprets the instructions of a program in storage and produces signals that act as commands to circuits
    c. communicates with input devices to initiate the transfer of results from storage
    d. all of the above

    *   *   *   *   *   *   *   *   *

(d) The control unit maintains order and controls all activity in the CPU. It directs the sequence of operations and interprets program instructions. It initiates the transfer of instructions, data, and results to and from storage.

3. The stored-program concept refers to
    a. wired control panels that are plugged into the computer at the beginning of a program
    b. instructions read into a computer using punched cards in discrete steps
    c. using the memory of the computer to store both data and the set of instructions required to manipulate that data
    d. maintaining programs in a file in case they are needed in the future

    *   *   *   *   *   *   *   *   *

(c) The stored-program concept was important to the development of the computer. Storing instructions and data in the computer's internal memory greatly expands its usefulness.

4. The part of a computer instruction that tells the computer unit what operation is to be performed is called the
    a. operand   c. register
    b. address   d. operation code

    *   *   *   *   *   *   *   *   *

(d) The operation code and the operand are the two basic parts of computer instructions. The operation code (op code) is the part that tells the control unit what operation is to be performed. The operand indicates the location of the data to be operated on.

5.   Devices that act as temporary holding areas for instruc-
     tions and data are called
     a. buffers   c. variables
     b. registers   d. addresses

     *   *   *   *   *   *   *   *   *

     (b) Registers, which are located in the CPU, receive data,
     hold the data, and transfer them very quickly when directed
     by the control unit. This speeds up the execution of
     instructions.

6.   The principle by which items stored in main memory can be
     read as many times as necessary is known as
     a. next-sequential-instruction feature
     b. stored program
     c. permanent memory
     d. non-destructive read/destructive write

     *   *   *   *   *   *   *   *   *

     (d) Non-destructive read/destructive write means that
     instructions or data can be read as many times as
     necessary. When data is written on top of the instruc-
     tions, the previous contents of the space are destroyed.

7.   A memory device that consists of magnetized spots resting
     on a thin film of semiconductor material is called
     a. semiconductor memory   c. domain memory
     b. bubble memory   d. magnetic core memory

     *   *   *   *   *   *   *   *   *

     (b) Bubble memory consists of magnetized dots (bubbles)
     that rest on a thin film of semiconductor material. Bubble
     memory is nonvolatile and does not require a constant
     source of power.

8.   When functions are built into the hardware of a computer
     they are placed in
     a. core memory   c. hardware memory
     b. biochips   d. read-only memory

     *   *   *   *   *   *   *   *   *

     (d) Read-only memory is the part of the computer hardware
     containing items that are wired into the computer. ROM
     cannot be erased or changed by regular program instruc-
     tions.

9.   Data represented in the computer by the electrical state of
      the machine's circuitry is represented in two states "on"
      or "off." This is called
      a. hexadecimal representation c. binary representation
      b. octal representation   d. none of the above

      *   *   *   *   *   *   *   *   *   *

      (c) Binary representation works on the base-2 number
      system. It works in a manner similar to the decimal
      number system.

10.   A fixed number of adjacent bits operated on as a unit is
      called
      a. a byte   c. a parity bit
      b. K   d. a check bit

      *   *   *   *   *   *   *   *   *   *

      (a) A byte is usually eight adjacent bits. This is the
      case whenever a computer accepts 8-bit characters.

TRUE/FALSE

1.   T   F   In order to use a computer effectively, the user
               should have a working knowledge of the computer's
               internal electronic circuitry.

2.   T   F   A computer program is a series of instructions.

3.   T   F   The operation code (op code) tells the control unit
               what function is to be performed.

4.   T   F   Most modern computers are stored-program computers.

5.   T   F   All storage considered part of the CPU is called a
               register.

6.   T   F   Parity can be changed at will by the user.

7.   T   F   If the power source fails, data stored in semicon-
               ductor memory is lost.

8.   T   F   Digital computers measure the continuous flow of
               physical or electrical states.

9.   T   F   PROM memory can be changed while ROM memory cannot.

10.   T   F   Cache memory is also referred to as high-speed
               buffer.

MATCHING

a.   dump   f.   binary
b.   octal   g.   PROM
c.   primary memory   h.   central processing unit
d.   register   i.   semiconductor memory
e.   EPROM   j.   program

1.   The control unit, the arithmetic/logic unit, and the pri-
     mary storage unit comprise the _____.

2.   An internal computer component used for temporary storage
     of an instruction or data is called a(n) _____.

3   Main memory or internal storage is also referred to as
     _____.

4.   Data representation in the computer is based on a(n)
     _____ system.

5.   A type of read-only memory that can be reprogrammed by
     users to meet unique needs is called _____.

6.   The type of primary storage (memory) device that requires a
     constant power source is _____.

7.   A set of instructions that tells the computer exactly what
     to do is a(n) _____.

8.   A printout of the contents of the computer's memory is
     called a(n) _____.

9.   A type of read-only memory that can be programmed only once
     to meet user needs is known as _____.

10. The number system that uses the digits zero through seven
     is known as _____ representation.

SHORT ANSWER

1.   What is the difference between ROM, PROM, and EPROM?

2.   How is the nondestructive read/destructive write operation similar to a tape recorder?

3.   What is a variable?

4.   What does it mean when characters are written in even parity? In odd parity?

5.   What is the difference betweeen digital and analog com-
     puters?

6.   What is ASCII?

7.   What is the difference between an op code and an operand?

8.   What are the functions of the ALU?

9.   What is meant by the term next-sequential-instruction
      feature?

10.   What is primary storage?

ANSWER KEY

True/False

1. F   3. T   5. F   7. T   9. F

Matching

1. h   3. c   5. e   7. j   9. g

Short Answer

1.   ROM is permanent and cannot be changed. PROM can be
      programmed to meet the user's needs, but only once. EPROM
      can be reprogrammed as many times as necessary.

3.   A variable is a name given to a storage location by a
      programmer. The term variable is used because the contents
      of the storage location may change while the address loca-
      tion will not.

5.   Digital computers operate on the basis of discrete "on" and "off" states represented by binary data. Analog computers measure the changes in continuous physical or electrical states.

7.   The op code tells the control unit what function is to be performed while the operand indicates the primary storage location of the data to be operated on.

9.   Next-sequential-instruction feature implies that all the instructions necessary to perform a complete operation will be stored in consecutive locations in memory.

Input and Output

KEY TERMS

Amount field – The field where a clerk manually inserts the amount of the check; used in the processing of bank checks.

Audio input system – See Voice recognition device.

Bar-code reader – A device used to read a bar code by means of reflected light, such as a scanner that reads the Universal Product Code on supermarket products.

Card punch – See Keypunch.

Cathode-ray tube (CRT) – A visual display device that receives electrical impulses and translates them into a picture on a television-like screen.

Chain printer – An output device that has the character set engraved in type and assembled in a chain that revolves horizontally past all print positions; prints when a print hammer (one for each column of the paper) presses the paper against an inked ribbon that presses against the characters on the print chain.

Character-at-a-time printer – Prints just one character of information at a time.

Clustered key-to-tape device – Several keyboards are tied to one or two magnetic-tape units.

Computer output microfilm (COM) – Miniature photographic images of output. Computer output is placed on magnetic tape which serves as the input to a microfilm processor.

Continuous form - A data-entry form, such as cash register tape, utilized by OCR devices.

Cut form - Data-entry form such as a phone or utility bill; used by OCR devices.

Daisy-wheel printer - An output device resembling an office typewriter; it employs a flat disk with petal-like projections with characters on the surfaces; printing occurs one character at a time.

Digit rows - The lower ten rows, numbers 0 through 9, that are found on an 80-column punched card.

Digitizer - An input device that allows for the input of two-dimensional images into computer memory; the images are traced in the X/Y plane and the coordinates are transformed into object form by the digitizer software.

Dot-matrix printer - A type of impact printer that creates characters through the use of dot-matrix patterns.

Drum printer - An output device consisting of a metal cylinder that contains rows of characters engraved across its surface; one line of print is produced with each rotation of the drum.

Eighty-column punched card - See Hollerith card.

Electronic drawing pen - See Light pen.

Electrostatic printer - A nonimpact printer in which electromagnetic impulses and heat are used to affix characters to paper.

Electrothermal printer - A nonimpact printer that uses a special heat sensitive paper and forms characters on the paper using heat.

Field - A meaningful item of data, such as a social security number.

Flexible diskette - A low-cost, random-access form of data storage made of plastic; a flexible magnetic disk currently made in 3 1/2-, 5 1/4-, and 8-inch diameter sizes.

Floppy diskette - See Flexible diskette.

Graphic display device – A visual-display device that projects output in the form of graphs and line drawings and accepts input from a keyboard or light pen.

Hard copy – Printed output.

Hollerith card – An 80-column punched card.

Hollerith code – A method of data representation where the placement of holes in 80-column punched cards represents numbers, letters, and special characters.

Impact printer – A printer that forms characters by physically striking print element, ribbon and paper together.

Ink-jet printer – A nonimpact printer that uses a stream of charged ink to form dot-matrix characters.

Intelligent terminal – A terminal with an internal processor that can be programmed to perform specified functions, such as data editing, data conversion, and control of other terminals.

Keypunch – A keyboard device that punches holes in a card to represent data.

Key-to-disk – Hardware designed to transfer data entered via a keyboard to magnetic disk or diskette.

Key-to-tape – Hardware designed to transfer data entered via a keyboard to magnetic tape.

Laser printer – A type of nonimpact printer that combines laser beams and electrophotographic technology to form images on paper.

Light pen – A pen-shaped object with a photoelectric cell at its end; used to draw lines on a visual-display screen.

Line-at-a-time printer – Prints an entire line of information at a time.

Machine language – The only set of instructions that a computer can execute directly; a code that designates the proper electrical states in the computer as combinations of 0s and 1s.

Magnetic-ink character recognition (MICR) device – A device that reads characters composed of magnetized particles; often used to sort checks for subsequent processing.

Mark-sensing – See Optical mark recognition.

Nonimpact printer – The use of heat, laser technology, or photographic techniques to print output.

"On us" field – The section of a check that contains the customer's checking account number.

Optical character – A special type of character that can be read by an optical-character reader.

Optical character recognition (OCR) – A capability of devices with electronic scanners that read numbers, letters, and other characters, and convert the optical images into appropriate electrical signals.

Optical-mark page reader – A device that senses marks on an OMR document as the document passes under a light source.

Optical-mark recognition (OMR) – Also mark sensing; a capability of devices with electronic scanners that read marks on a page and convert the optical images into appropriate electrical signals.

Plotter – An output device that converts data emitted from the CPU into graphic form; produces hard-copy output.

Point-of-sale (POS) system – A computerized system that records information required for such things as inventory control and accounting at the point where a good is sold; see also Source data automation.

Print-wheel printer – An output device consisting of 120 print wheels, each containing 48 characters. The print wheels rotate until the entire line is in the appropriate position, then a hammer presses the paper against the print wheel.

Printer – A device used to produce permanent (hard-copy) computer output; impact printers are designed to work mechanically; nonimpact printers use heat, laser, and chemical technology.

Printer-keyboard – An output device similar to an office typewriter; prints one character at a time and is controlled by a program stored in the CPU of the computer.

Punched card – An updated form of sequential storage in which the data is represented by the presence or absence of strategically placed holes.

Soft copy – Data displayed on a CRT screen; not a permanent record; contrast with hard copy.

Source-data automation – The use of special equipment to collect data at its source.

Stand-alone key-to-tape device – A self-contained unit that takes the place of a key punch device.

Touch-sensitive screen – A display screen that serves as an input device; the display is divided into a grid and sensors are placed in the screen to allow the terminal to sense being touched; a method of input that does not require the use of a keyboard.

Touch-tone devices – Terminals used with ordinary telephone lines to transmit data.

Train printer – See Chain printer.

Transit field – The section of a check, preprinted with magnetic ink, that includes the bank number.

Unit record – One set of information; the amount of data on one punched card.

Universal Product Code (UPC) – A code consisting of ten pairs of vertical bars that represent the manufacturer's iden-tity and the identity code of the item; commonly used on most grocery items.

Visual display terminal – A terminal capable of receiving output on a cathode-ray tube (CRT) and, with special provisions, is capable of transmitting data through a keyboard.

Voice synthesizer – The output portion of a voice com-munication system; used to provide verbal output from the com-puter system to the user.

Voice-recognition module (VRM) – A module, or dictionary, that contains the words and phrases that can be recognized by a voice-recognition device.

Voice-recognition system – The input portion of a com-munication system; used to provide verbal input from the user to the computer system.

Wand reader – A device used in reading source data repre-sented in optical bar-code form.

Wire-matrix printer – See Dot-matrix printer.

Xerographic printer – A type of nonimpact printer that uses printing methods similar to those used in common xerographic copying machines.

Zone rows – The upper three rows, numbered 12, 11, and 0, that are found on an 80-column punched card.

SUMMARY

Computer input can take many forms. One of the earliest forms of computer input was the punched card. The standard punched card contains 12 rows and 80 columns. The card is divided into digit rows, zone rows, and the print zone. When a punched card contains all the information pertaining to a transaction, it is called a unit record.

To overcome the limitations of punched cards, key-to-tape and key-to-disk machines were developed. Data is entered directly onto the tape or disk in the form of magnetized spots. An increasingly popular data-entry system is the key-to-diskette system. A floppy disk is used instead of a conventional disk.

Since data entry is often the slowest part of computer processing, occasionally data is collected when and where it is generated. This is called source-data automation. Several devices have been created to facilitate the collection of data in different situations.

Magnetic-ink character readers are used to process bank checks. Optical-mark recognition is used in the grading of multiple-choice exams. Bar code readers are used in grocery stores to read the Universal Product Code that appears on grocery items. Optical character readers operate on the same principle as optical mark readers, only they distinguish the shape of the character rather than its position on the paper.

Several different terminals have been developed that will collect data. Some perform other functions as well. Point-of-sale terminals operate as cash registers and data-entry stations. Touch-tone devices can be coupled with telephones to operate as data-entry stations. Voice recognition devices translate audio input into computer signals. Voice recognition is limited in use because of the many variations in people's voices. Intelligent terminals can process data.

Computer printers print processed data in a form that humans can understand. This permanent readable copy of computer output is often referred to as hard copy. To produce hard copy, printers receive electronic signals from the central processing unit.

Printers may be divided into impact and nonimpact printers. In an impact printer, electronic signals from the CPU activate print elements which are pressed against paper. Nonimpact printers have newer technology and use heat, laser technology, or photographic techniques to print output. There are several types of impact and nonimpact printers.

Visual display devices are output devices that display data on cathode-ray tubes (CRTs) which are similar to television screens. These terminals supply soft copy output. This means that the screen image is not a permanent record of what is shown. Graphic display devices are used to display drawings as well as characters on a screen.

Specialized output devices provide output in specialized forms. Plotters convert data from the CPU into graphic form. Computer output microfilm (COM) consists of photographic images produced in miniature by the computer. Voice synthesizers provide verbal responses, or output, to the computer user.

STRUCTURED LEARNING

1.   Representation of alphabetic and special characters on a punched card requires
     a.   using zone rows only
     b.   using zone bits
     c.   using the digit rows only
     d.   none of the above

     *   *   *   *   *   *   *   *   *

     (d) The digit rows on the punched card can represent any number--zero through nine. When combined with zone punches, alphabetic and special characters can be represented.

2.   Which is a major difficulty associated with the use of
      punched cards?
      a.   Records are limited to 80 columns in length.
      b.   When less than an entire card is needed for a record,
            the remaining space is wasted.
      c.   The display section at the top of the card wastes
            valuable space that could be used to encode more data.
      d.   both a and d
      e.   none of the above

      *   *   *   *   *   *   *   *   *

      (d) Standard punched cards provide no flexibility as to
      card length since all cards contain 80 columns. Problems
      are encountered because of limited record size or wasted
      space if the entire card is not needed.

3.   Point-of-sale terminals
      a.   speed the checkout process at supermarkets
      b.   often use wands to read the UPC
      c.   can be used to collect useful inventory and sales
            information
      d.   all of the above

      *   *   *   *   *   *   *   *   *

      (d) POS terminals can effectively do all of these tasks.
      Supermarkets that use POS terminals can operate more effi-
      ciently since checkout time is reduced and inventory
      control can be collected automatically using POS terminals.

4.   Soft-copy output is produced by a(n)
      a.   POS terminal   d.   graphic display device
      b.   MICR   e.   both c and d
      c.   chain printer

      *   *   *   *   *   *   *   *   *

      (d) Soft-copy output is produced only temporarily by this
      device on a screen similar to a television screen.

5.   Terminals that collect data at their source and transmit
      them to a central computer for processing are called
      a.   graphic-display terminals   c.   remote terminals
      b.   CAT terminals   d.   transit terminals

      *   *   *   *   *   *   *   *   *

(c) Generally, data is transmitted over telecommunication equipment from remote terminals to a central computer for processing. The many types of remote terminals available can expand the applications of a computer system.

6.   Printers that receive electronic signals from the central processing unit that activate print elements which are pressed against paper are called
   a.   impact printers   c.   hard copy printers
   b.   nonimpact printers   d.   xerographic printers

   *   *   *   *   *   *   *   *   *

(a) Nonimpact printers use heat, laser technology, or photographic techniques to print output. Xerographic printers are a type of nonimpact printer. All printers produce hard copy.

7.   The fastest printers are broadly classified as
   a.   character-at-a-time printers
   b.   line-at-a-time printers
   c.   nonimpact printers
   d.   impact printers

   *   *   *   *   *   *   *   *   *

(c) Nonimpact printers employ techniques requiring less mechanical movement than impact printers. This speeds the printing of output.

8.   Which types of printers are based on a design principle similar to that of a football or basketball scoreboard?
   a.   dot-matrix and daisy-wheel printers
   b.   dot-matrix and wire-matrix printers
   c.   chain and drum printers
   d.   ink-jet and laser printers

   *   *   *   *   *   *   *   *   *

(b) The matrix is a rectangle composed of pins. Certain combinations of pins are activated to represent characters.

9. Which is true when using computer output microfilm?
    a. The cost of producing additional copies is prohibitive.
    b. The computer can be used to retrieve the microfilmed data.
    c. The output can be made highly readable using forms-overlay to print headings and superimpose lines.
    d. all of the above

    *   *   *   *   *   *   *   *   *

    (c) COM is an effective technique for sorting large quantities of data at a low cost. The use of forms-overlay to structure the data stored on the microfilm improves the readability and retrieval of data.

10. Which of the following does not apply to OCR devices?
    a. Human error is reduced.
    b. Symbols used are both human- and machine-readable.
    c. They are no longer being used in stores.
    d. They are best suited for low-volume processing.

    *   *   *   *   *   *   *   *   *

    (d) Because OCR devices reduce human error while inputting data that is both human-readable and machine-readable, they are extremely useful for processing high-volume transactions.

TRUE/FALSE

1. T F A major difficulty associated with the use of punched cards is the 80-column limitation.

2. T F Not all punched cards contain 80 vertical columns.

3. T F Keypunching, though slow, is the least expensive operation in either computer or punched-card systems.

4. T F The unit record is a complete record containing all necessary data about a transaction on one punched card.

5. T F Key-to-disk, key-to-tape, and key-to-diskette systems are less expensive than punched card output.

6.   T   F   Optical-mark recognition uses an optical-mark page
               reader that automatically translates data into
               machine language.

7.   T   F   Data can be fed into an OCR either in a continuous
               form such as a cash-register tape or in cut form
               such as utility bills.

8.   T   F   Intelligent terminals have the same kinds of com-
               ponents as full-sized computers, and they are unlim-
               ited in their storage capacity.

9.   T   F   Graphic display terminals are used when hard-copy
               output is desired, and plotters are used when only
               soft-copy output is necessary.

10.   T   F   Printers produce processed data in a form humans can
               read.

MATCHING

a.   transit field   f.   soft copy
b.   plotter   g.   light wand
c.   light pen   h.   OMR
d.   impact   i.   on us field
e.   digit row   j.   graphic display device

1.   Preprinted on all checks to identify the bank on which the
      check is drawn is the _____.

2.   Data or pictures displayed on a graphic display device can
      be altered using a(n) _____.

3.   Output which appears on a display screen is called _____.

4.   A device that converts data emitted from the CPU into hard-
      copy graphic form is a(n) _____.

5.   _____ is used in grading multiple-choice exams.

6.   The _____ is preprinted on checks to identify the cus-
      tomer's checking account number.

7.   A device that converts data emitted from the CPU into soft
      copy graphic form is a(n) _____.

8.   The section of a 12-by-80 punched card which is used to represent numbers is called _____.

9.   A(n) _____ is used to read bar codes.

10. A printer that relies on electronic signals to activate print elements which are pressed against paper is called a(n) _____ printer.

SHORT ANSWER

1.   What is meant by source-data automation?

2.   Discuss two limitations of punched cards.

3.   What is a unit record?

4.   Name several impact printers.

5.   What are some of the advantages of CRTs as output devices
      over printers?

6.   How are magnetic-ink characters interpreted by the com-
      puter?

7.   What are some advantages of using computer output micro-
      film?

8.   How are optical marks read by the optical-mark page reader?

9.   For what uses are voice recognition systems suitable?

10.   What is a touch-tone device?

ANSWER KEY

True/False

1. T   3. F   5. F   7. T   9. F

Matching

1. a   3. f   5. h   7. j   9. g

Short Answer

1. Source-data automation involves the collection of data
    about an event in computer-readable form when and where the
    event takes place. The elimination of intermediate steps
    used in preparing card input improves the speed, accuracy,
    and efficiency of data-processing operations.

3. A unit record is a punched card that contains all necessary
    data about a transaction.

5. ● they can display output faster than printers
    ● they are quieter in operation

7. ● data can store compactly reducing space requirements and
      storage costs
    ● both character and graphic output can be recorded
    ● the cost of producing additional copies is low

9. They are suitable for low-volume, highly formal input and
    output. Users may enter data into the computer by
    "training" the computer to understand their voices and
    vocabulary.

Storage
Devices

KEY TERMS

Access mechanism – The physical device that positions the read/write head of a direct-access storage device over a particular track.

Blocked records – Records grouped on magnetic tape or magnetic disk to reduce the number of interrecord gaps and more fully utilize the storage medium.

Block – In block-structured programming languages, a section of program coding treated as a unit.

Charge-coupled device (CCD) – A storage device that is made of silicon; is nearly one hundred times faster than magnetic bubbles.

Cylinder – All tracks on a magnetic disk that are accessible by the read/write heads with one movement, or positioning, of the access mechanism.

Density – The number of characters that can be stored on one inch of tape; storage capacity of the tape depends in part on its density.

Direct-access storage – A method of storing data whereby they can be retrieved in any order, at random.

Disk address – The method used to uniquely identify a data record on a magnetic disk; consists of the disk surface number, the track number, and the record number.

Disk drive – The mechanical device used to rotate a disk pack during data transmission; common speeds range between 40 and 1,000 revolutions per second.

Disk pack – A stack of magnetic disks.

Flexible disk – Also known as diskette, or floppy disk; a low-cost random-access form of data storage made of plastic; a flexible magnetic disk currently made in 3½-, 5¼-, and 8-inch diameter sizes.

Interblock gap (IBG) – A space on magnetic tape that facilitates processing; records are grouped together and separated by interblock gaps.

Interrecord gap (IRG) – A space that separates records stored on magnetic tape; allows the tape drive to regain speed during processing.

Josephson Junction – A primary storage unit that, when completed, will be housed in liquid helium to reduce the resistance to the flow of electricity that currently exists in semiconductor memory.

Laser storage system – A secondary storage device using laser technology to encode data onto a metallic surface; usually used for mass storage.

Magnetic disk – A storage medium consisting of a metal platter coated on both sides with a magnetic recording material upon which data is stored in the form of magnetized spots; suitable for direct-access processing.

Magnetic tape – A storage medium consisting of a narrow strip upon which spots of iron-oxide are magnetized to represent data; a sequential storage medium.

Mass storage – High-density magnetic tapes or disks used to store infrequently used data while retaining accessibility.

Optical disk – Also known as a laser disk; stores data as the presence or absence of a pit burned into the surface of the disk by a laser beam.

Primary storage – Also internal storage, primary memory, main storage; the section of the CPU that holds instructions, data, and intermediate and final results during processing.

RAM (random-access memory) chips – The most popular of the microchips; a continuous supply of power is needed.

Read/write head – An electromagnet used as a component of a tape or disk drive; in reading, it detects magnetized areas and translates them into electrical pulses; in writing, it magnetizes appropriate areas, thereby erasing data stored previously.

Secondary storage – Also known as external or auxiliary storage; supplements primary storage but operates at slower speeds.

Sequential-access storage – Auxiliary storage from which records must be read, one after another, in a fixed sequence, until the needed data are located; for example, magnetic tape.

Tape cartridge – See Tape cassette.

Tape cassette – A sequential-access storage medium (similar to cassettes used in audio recording) used in small computer systems for high-density digital recording.

Tape drive – A device that moves tape past a read/write head.

Track – A horizontal row stretching the length of a magnetic tape on which data can be recorded; one of a series of concentric circles on the surface of a magnetic disk; one of a series of circular bands on a magnetic drum.

SUMMARY

Auxiliary or secondary storage is not part of the CPU. Computer systems rely on secondary storage for storing large volumes of data more cheaply than they could be stored in main memory.

Data in secondary storage can be accessed sequentially or directly. Magnetic tape is an example of sequential-access storage. This means that in order to read a record at the end of the tape, all the records preceding it must be read first. Records on magnetic tape are blocked to reduce blank spaces on the tape. Data are stored on the tape as magnetized spots in a horizontal track. Standard magnetic tape is one-half inch wide on ten-inch reels. It is also available in cassettes and cartridges.

Magnetic tape offers much more flexibility than punched cards. It has unlimited record length, is reusable, and is inexpensive. It must be kept in a controlled environment, however.

Magnetic disks (made of metal) provide direct-access storage. This implies that any desired record can be accessed immediately without previously processing any other record. Data are stored on a disk as magnetized spots on a concentric track. Disks are permanently mounted on a central shaft to form disk packs.

Floppy disks resemble hard disks but are made of plastic. Because they are flexible, they can be handled or even mailed. Floppy disks are typically used as storage for mini- and micro-computer systems.

Mass storage, though slower than disk or tape, allows rapid access to data that are used infrequently. Some types of mass storage systems use a high-density cassette tape while others use floppy disks.

Advances are being made rapidly in the area of auxiliary storage. Recent advances include charge-coupled devices and laser storage systems.

STRUCTURED LEARNING

1.   Which of the following is not considered to be secondary storage?
      a.   magnetic tapes   c.   magnetic bubbles
      b.   punched cards   d.   magnetic disks

      *   *   *   *   *   *   *   *   *

      (c) Magnetic bubbles are an innovative replacement for magnetic cores within the CPU. They are faster and smaller than magnetic cores.

2.   Which of the following is a major advantage of direct-
     access storage devices?
     a. They do not need to be directly linked to the computer.
     b. Data can be located much faster than data stored on
         sequential-access media.
     c. Data are stored in human-readable form.
     d. none of the above

     *   *   *   *   *   *   *   *   *

     (b) Direct-access devices allow rapid location of data
     because the read/write head can be correctly positioned
     over the appropriate track without searching all other
     tracks. The programmer simply needs to specify the disk
     surface number, track number, and record number.

3.   Individual records on magnetic tape are separated by
     a. parity bits   c. read/write coils
     b. interrecord gaps   d. EBCDIC

     *   *   *   *   *   *   *   *   *

     (b) To make certain that each record is read correctly,
     records are separated by interrecord gaps. When the
     read/write head detects an IRG, it stops reading the tape.
     The remaining portion of the IRG allows the tape drive to
     gain speed when it is necessary to read the next record.

4.   The purpose of IRGs is to
     a. separate individual records
     b. fully utilize the tape
     c. allow the tape drive to gain speed
     d. both a and c
     e. both b and c

     *   *   *   *   *   *   *   *   *

     (d) The separation of records is important for accurate
     data processing. The beginning of an IRG signals the end
     of a record while the remaining portion of the IRG allows
     the tape device to gain speed when it is necessary to read
     the next record.

5.   Storage capacity of a magnetic tape is determined by the
      tape's
      a.   record length   d.   interblock gap
      b.   density   e.   interrecord gap
      c.   drive unit speed

      *   *   *   *   *   *   *   *   *

      (b) Tape density refers to the number of characters that
      can be stored on each inch of magnetic tape. The greater
      the density, the greater the storage capacity of the tape.

6.   Data stored on magnetic disk are accessed by
      a.   disk surface number   c.   record number
      b.   track number   d.   all of the above

      *   *   *   *   *   *   *   *   *

      (d) The disk surface number, track number, and record
      number allow data recorded on a magnetic disk to be
      directly accessed. Direct access to data allows the devel-
      opment of online applications which require rapid response.

7.   Which of the following is not an advantage resulting from
      the use of magnetic disks?
      a.   relatively low cost
      b.   fast access time
      c.   rapid response to inquiries
      d.   sequential- or direct-access processing capabilities

      *   *   *   *   *   *   *   *   *

      (a) Disk storage is more expensive than punched-card,
      paper-tape, or magnetic-tape storage. The capabilities
      provided by magnetic disk often offset the increase in
      cost.

8.   Which of the following is true of floppy disks?
      a.   they are inexpensive   c.   they are flexible
      b.   they may be reused   d.   all of the above

      *   *   *   *   *   *   *   *   *

      (d) All of the above are true of floppy disks. They also
      have many of the same capabilities as magnetic disks.

9.   Mass storage devices
      a.   are sequential-access devices
      b.   provide storage for vast quantities of data but are
            expensive
      c.   commonly use cassette-type cartridge tape and floppy
            disk systems
      d.   allow access to data as rapidly as magnetic disks

      *   *   *   *   *   *   *   *

      (c) Mass storage devices provide access to data at a rela-
      tively rapid rate. Cassette-type cartridge tape and floppy
      disk systems permit direct access inexpensively.

10.   Which of the following is not true of laser storage
      systems?
      a.   make patterns on a polyester sheet
      b.   are more expensive than standard magnetic media
      c.   are not susceptible to power failure
      d.   are resistant to alteration

      *   *   *   *   *   *   *   *

      (b) Laser storage can store characters at one-tenth the
      cost of standard magnetic media.

TRUE/FALSE

1.   T   F   Computer systems can use either direct-access
                storage or sequential-access storage, but not both
                within the same system at the same time.

2.   T   F   The most common method of representing data on tape
                uses a nine-track coding scheme.

3.   T   F   A disadvantage of magnetic tape is that it is a
                relatively expensive storage medium.

4.   T   F   The number of cylinders in a disk pack is equal to
                the number of tracks.

5.   T   F   A tape drive runs continuously while data are being
                read.

6.   T   F   Magnetic tape, like punched cards, limits record
                length to 80 columns.

7.   T F   The density of the data on a tape determines how
             fast the data can be transferred from the tape to
             the CPU.

8.   T F   If a disk pack contains 11 disks, there would be 22
             recording surfaces.

9.   T F   Disk records are separated by gaps similar to the
             interrecord gaps on magnetic tape.

10.   T F   Floppy disks were originally introduced as a medium
             to replace punched cards.

MATCHING

a.	floppy disks	f.	mass storage
b.	interrecord gaps	g.	access mechanism
c.	tracks	h.	optical
d.	secondary	i.	disk address
e.	density	j.	rhodium

1.   _____ storage is not part of the CPU.

2.   Laser, also known as _____ disks, are much faster than
     hard disks but are still fairly slow when compared to
     random-access memory.

3.   Data stored on a magnetic disk is located by disk surface
     number, track number, and record number. This information
     constitutes a(n) _____.

4.   Magnetic tape is divided into nine horizontal channels
     called _____.

5.   The number of characters that can be stored on one inch of
     tape is called the _____ of the tape.

6.   _____ is used to coat a polyester sheet in a laser
     storage system.

7.   Read/write heads on a magnetic disk are positioned over the
     appropriate track by the _____.

8.   Individual records on magnetic tape are separated by
     _____.

9. Since small computer systems may not need a large amount of auxiliary storage, _____ have been developed.

10. To meet the need for cost-effective storage of large amounts of data for direct-access processing, _____ devices were developed.

SHORT ANSWER

1. Distinguish between primary storage and secondary storage.

2. Differentiate between sequential-access and direct-access storage.

3. What is the function of interblock gaps?

4.   What are the advantages of magnetic tape storage?

5.   What is the primary advantage of magnetic disk storage?

6.   Why are backup capabilities important when magnetic disk
      storage is used?

7.   Why were mass storage media developed?

8.   What are the characteristics of charge-coupled devices?

9.   What are the trends in storage media technology?

10. What information is necessary to access a specific record
     stored on a magnetic disk?

ANSWER KEY

True/False

1. T   3. F   5. F   7. T   9. T

Matching

1. d   3. i   5. e   7. g   9. a

Short Answer

1.   Primary storage is considered part of the CPU while secon-
      dary storage is external to the CPU. Secondary storage is
      less expensive than primary storage.

3.   Interblock gaps are used with magnetic tape to limit wasted
      space and to allow more records to be stored on one reel.
      Since the tape drive spends less time stopping and
      starting, processing occurs more rapidly and efficiently.

5.   Magnetic disk storage allows a great deal of processing
      flexibility since it is a direct-access medium. Disk
      storage is often used for online file updating and for when
      there are frequent inquiries into the data files.

7.   Mass storage devices were developed to inexpensively store
      large amounts of data that needed to be rapidly accessed.

9.   The trends are toward designing storage media that are less
      expensive, faster, and smaller than those media in current
      use.

Microcomputers

KEY TERMS

Communication channel – A medium for carrying data from one location to another.

Computer store – A retail store that sells computers and is structured to appeal to the small business person or personal user.

Distributed data processing – Data processing that is done at a site other than that of the central computer.

Electronic bulletin board – A communication network used to send messages to members of a group which share a common interest; uses existing communication networks.

Fixed disk – A magnetic disk system used on microcomputers that is a sealed unit that cannot be accessed by the user; relatively low-priced, reliable, secure, small in size, and has large storage capacity.

Game paddle – An input device that is normally used with microcomputers for game applications; it is used to position a figure that is required to move across or up and down the display screen.

Hard magnetic disks – Magnetic disks that can be used on microcomputer systems; they are found in two configurations—fixed disk and removable disk.

Joystick - An input device that is normally used with microcomputers for game applications; it is used to position some object, such as a cursor, on the display screen.

Microprocessor - The CPU of a microcomputer.

Mouse - A small device used primarily on microcomputers for the positioning of the cursor; its primary advantage is that it eliminates a great deal of typing for some applications.

Parallelism - The process of simultaneous data movement through a number of communication channels on a computer system.

Peripheral device - A device that attaches to the CPU, such as secondary storage devices and input/output devices.

Removable disk - A hard magnetic disk unit that can be used on a microcomputer for secondary storage; allows for one disk to be removed and another inserted.

Stand-alone mode - A strategy that allows the user to keep applications in a local mode, allowing no access to remote computer facilities, thus avoiding problems of online use.

Telecommuting - Computer hookups between offices and homes, thereby allowing employees to work at home.

SUMMARY

The evolution of microcomputers has differed greatly from that of mainframe computers. Microcomputers were developed by individuals using their own financial resources and innovative ideas. Mainframes were developed through large-scale research efforts. Microcomputers rose rapidly in acceptance and popularity. Since the introduction of microcomputers in 1975, total sales have reached over five million units. It took mainframe computers nearly fifteen years to reach the same level of acceptance. Because of the versatility and widespread acceptance of microcomputers, they have many current and potential uses.

One-third of all personal computers are located in private offices where they are used for many applications. One of the most popular uses of personal computers in business is for word processing. Word processing is the manipulation of text data to achieve a desired output. Personal computers are also used for telecommuting. Telecommuting involves computer hookups between offices and homes that allow employees to work at home.

Telecommuting allows firms to employ labor resources that might not otherwise be available, like homemakers and handicapped people.

Personal computers have led to the growth of computer stores. These stores are structured to appeal to owners of small businesses and personal computer users.

The heart of a microcomputer is the microprocessor, a single integrated circuit that contains an arithmetic/logic unit as well as control capability for memory and input/output access. The prefix "micro" refers to size and cost and not capability.

A microprocessor and a mainframe CPU perform nearly iden- tical functions, but the manner in which these functions are performed differs. The architectural design of a mainframe per- mits larger instruction sets, access to more memory in a single step, and greater speed in processing. Microcomputers have smaller registers than mainframes, and they allow for only one user at a time. Microcomputers use only one communication chan- nel to communicate with peripherals while mainframes use a con- cept called parallelism. Microcomputers are powerful in proportion to their size; sometimes their power is equal to that of early mainframes.

Storage capacity of microcomputers is limited, so peripheral methods of storage have been developed for use with micros. Magnetic tape cassettes, cartridges, and floppy disks are all used with microcomputers. Data storage on floppy disks varies according to the density of storage on the surface of the disk and the side of the disk on which data is stored. Hard magnetic disks provide more storage than floppy disks. Hard disks come in two varieties: fixed and removable.

The most common type of input/output device used with a microcomputer is a monitor. Monitors allow the user to view information before sending it to the microprocessor for proc- essing. They also allow the user to view information sent from the microprocessor. Information may be either characters or graphics. Monitors may be monochrome, color, RBG, or com- bination TV/monitors.

Joysticks and game paddles on microcomputers generally are used for game applications. A mouse is used to position the cursor on a computer monitor. It eliminates a great deal of keyboard typing.

When introduced, microcomputers were envisioned for use in homes and small businesses. Recently, however, they have been making their way into the management information systems of large companies. They are used in a stand-alone mode to aid in decision making, and they are being used for distributed processing and communication networks.

STRUCTURED LEARNING

1.   The early development of microcomputers occurred mainly due to the contributions of
      a.   scientists and universities
      b.   government agencies
      c.   individuals or small businesses
      d.   corporations which funded large-scale research

      *   *   *   *   *   *   *   *   *

      (c) The development of microcomputers is due largely to the efforts of individuals and small companies using their own financial resources. Entrepreneurs willing to risk their personal finances on the ideas in which they believed were involved in developing micros.

2.   The use of personal computers in small businesses has led to a new phenomenon known as telecommuting which
      a.   is based on computer hookups between offices and homes and allows employees to work at home
      b.   enables firms to employ labor resources that might not otherwise be available
      c.   employs commuters who find the rising costs of gasoline prohibitive
      d.   all of the above

      *   *   *   *   *   *   *   *   *

      (d) Many experiments with telecommuting are now in progress. By offering the telecommuting option to employees who want to stay home, many companies have reduced their employee turnover.

3. A single integrated circuit that contains an arithmetic/logic unit as well as control capabilities for memory and input/output access is
   a. a microprocessor
   b. a communication channel
   c. a mainframe CPU
   d. still in the process of being developed

*   *   *   *   *   *   *   *   *   *

(a) A microprocessor controls the sequence of operations and the arithmetic and logical operation as well as storing data, instructions, and intermediate final results in a microcomputer much the same as the CPU does on a mainframe computer.

4. A difference between a microcomputer and a mainframe is
   a. a microcomputer costs more than a mainframe
   b. a microcomputer is limited to one user with one communication channel
   c. microcomputers use parallelism
   d. a mainframe has a smaller word size than most microcomputers

*   *   *   *   *   *   *   *   *   *

(b) A microcomputer is limited to one user because only one communication channel is used to communicate with the computer's peripheral devices. Because only one channel is used, the software required to run the computer's operating system is less complex.

5. Which of the following is not true of microcomputers?
   a. Some microcomputers are very powerful in proportion to their size.
   b. Some microcomputers equal the power of early mainframes.
   c. Microcomputers require water coolant systems to keep their CPUs from overheating.
   d. Microcomputers can sit on a small desk or table top.

*   *   *   *   *   *   *   *   *

(c) Some early mainframe computers had to be water cooled to prevent overheating. They required air-conditioned rooms and were very expensive compared to today's micros.

6.   As an alternative method of storage, floppy disks
      a.   have become the most widely used form of peripheral
           storage
      b.   allow data to be accessed directly
      c.   vary in storage capacity depending upon the density of
           the disk
      d.   all of the above

      *   *   *   *   *   *   *   *   *

      (d) Floppy disks are faster in accessing data than cassette
      tapes or cartridges. They may store data on one or both
      sides of a disk and may be single or double in density.

7.   A disk that is a totally sealed unit with no user access
      is a
      a.   fixed disk   c.   floppy diskette
      b.   removable disk   d.   flexible disk

      *   *   *   *   *   *   *   *   *

      (a) A removable disk is a type of hard disk that allows the
      user to remove the disk and insert another. Flexible disk
      and floppy diskette are two different names for the same
      type of floppy disk.

8.   The most common type of input/output device is a
      a.   mouse   c.   monitor
      b.   game paddle   d.   joystick

      *   *   *   *   *   *   *   *   *

      (c) Monitors allow the user to view information before
      sending it to the microprocessor. They also allow the user
      to view information sent from the microprocessor. Almost
      every microcomputer is used with a monitor.

9.   Large companies are beginning to use microcomputers in
      a.   decision making   c.   distributed processing
      b.   a stand-alone mode   d.   all of the above

      *   *   *   *   *   *   *   *   *

      (d) Microcomputers were first envisioned for use in the home
      and small businesses. The current trend, though, is to use
      micros in large businesses in all of the above ways and
      many more.

10. An existing communications network that sends messages to various user groups is called
     a.   distributed processing
     b.   an electronic bulletin board
     c.   a communication channel
     d.   none of the above

     *   *   *   *   *   *   *   *   *

     (b) Electronic bulletin boards are growing in popularity. They provide information on a number of topics to users. Information relating to specific user groups or to all users can be sent over an electronic communication network.

TRUE/FALSE

1.   T   F   The evolution of microcomputers has closely followed the evolution of mainframes.

2.   T   F   Profitable applications of microcomputers are found in small businesses and in the professions.

3.   T   F   Computer stores are structured to appeal to large corporations.

4.   T   F   The heart of the microcomputer is the control unit.

5.   T   F   Registers in microcomputers are located in peripheral storage.

6.   T   F   Mainframe computers use a concept called parallelism to allow for what appears to be simultaneous data movement through a number of communication channels.

7.   T   F   Data storage on floppy disks varies according to the density of storage on the surface of the disk.

8.   T   F   Hard disks come in two varieties: fixed and non-fixed.

9.   T   F   Personal computers that have no access to remote computer facilities are said to be in a stand-alone mode.

10. T   F   An electronic bulletin board sets up a new communication network to send messages to user groups.

MATCHING

a.   computer store
b.   communication channel
c.   monitor
d.   microprocessor
e.   removable disk

f.   telecommuting
g.   electronic bulletin
     board
h.   parallelism
i.   stand-alone mode
j.   mouse

1.   A hand held input device that positions the cursor on the screen is called a(n) _____ .

2.   _____ is based on computer hookups between offices and homes that allow employees to work at home.

3.   With the emergence of the home computer concept, a new retailing phenomenon has evolved which is called the _____ .

4.   At the heart of the microcomputer is the _____ , a single integrated circuit.

5.   Microcomputers are limited to only one user because only one _____ is used to communicate with the computer's peripheral devices.

6.   The fixed disk is a totally sealed unit with no user access, while the _____ allows for one disk to be removed and another inserted.

7.   Many companies are using microcomputers in their day-to-day activities to perform tasks in a(n) _____ .

8.   The most common type of input/output device used with microcomputers is a(n) _____ .

9.   Mainframes use a concept called _____ to allow what appears to be simultaneous data movement through a number of communication channels.

10. A(n) _____ uses an existing communication network to send messages to various user groups.

SHORT ANSWER

1. Briefly describe the evolution of microcomputers.

2. What are some areas of application for microcomputers?

3. How have microcomputers affected the growth of computer stores?

4. How do microprocessors and mainframe computers differ in the way they process data?

5.   Why do microcomputers allow only one user at a time?

6.   How does the processing power of micros compare to early mainframes?

7.   How have the different storage capabilities of floppy disks affected disk drive compatibility?

8.   What are some positive features of fixed disks?

9.   What are the four categories into which monitors can be
     divided?

10.   What are some of the stand-alone applications for which
      microcomputers are being used in large corporations?

ANSWER KEY

True/False

1. F   3. F   5. F   7. T   9. T

Matching

1. j   3. a   5. b   7. i   9. h

Short Answer

1.   The first microcomputers were developed by individuals or
     small businesses using their own financial resources. The
     first microcomputer was introduced around 1975. People
     involved in developing microcomputers were entrepreneurs
     willing to risk their personal finances. The micros
     achieved rapid acceptance and are growing in use in many
     areas in businesses and homes.

3.   Until recently, personal computing was primarily a mail-
      order business. Products were shipped directly from manu-
      facturer to user. With the emergence of personal com-
      puters, computer stores have evolved. The stores appeal to
      owners of small businesses and personal computer users.

5.   Microcomputers are limited to one user because only one
      communication channel is used to communicate with the com-
      puter's peripheral devices. Mainframes use a concept
      called parallelism that allows for what appears to be
      simultaneous data movement through a number of com-
      munication channels.

7.   Some disk drives are designed to operate on single-sided
      disks only, while others operate on double-sided disks. A
      disk drive that can operate on a single density disk
      usually cannot operate on a double density disk. It is
      best to check out the disk drive capabilities before
      purchasing a disk to use with the drive unit.

9.   ● monochrome
      ● color
      ● RGB (red, green, blue)
      ● combination TV/monitor

Telecom- munications

KEY TERMS

Analog transmission – Transmission of data over communication channels in a continuous wave form.

Automatic teller machine (ATM) – Remote terminals that allow bank customers to communicate with the bank's central computer; user can perform such functions as check account balances, transfer funds, make deposits, withdrawals, and loan payments.

Bandwidth – The range, or width, of the frequencies available for transmission on a given channel.

Broad-band channels – Communication channels that can transmit data at rates of up to 120,000 bits per second; for example, laser beams and microwaves.

Buffer – Storage used to compensate for a difference in the rate of flow of data, or time of occurrence of events, when transmitting data from one device to another.

Channel – A limited-capacity computer that takes over the tasks of input and output in order to free the CPU to handle internal processing operations.

Communication channel – A medium for carrying data from one location to another.

Concentrator – A device that systematically allocates communication channels among several terminals.

Data buffering – Reading data into a separate storage unit normally contained in the control unit of the input/output subsystem.

Data communication – The electronic transmission of data from one site to another, usually over communication channels such as telephone/telegraph lines or microwaves.

Data set – A grouping of related records; also called a file.

Datacom handlers – See Multiplexer and Concentrator.

Demodulation – The process of retrieving data from a modulated carrier wave.

Digital transmission – The transmission of data as distinct "on"/"off" pulses.

Distributed data processing (DDP) – Data processing that is done at a site other than that of the central computer.

Electronic funds transfer (EFT) – A cashless method of paying for services or goods; the amounts of the two parties involved in the transaction are adjusted by electronic communication between computers.

Electronic mail – The transmission of messages at high speeds over telecommunication facilities.

Front-end processor – A small CPU serving as an interface between a large CPU and peripheral devices.

Full-duplex – A type of communication channel capable of the most versatile mode of data transmission; can transmit data in both directions simultaneously.

Grade – The range, or width, of the frequencies available for data transmission on a given channel.

Half-duplex – A type of communication channel through which communication can occur in both directions, but in only one direction at a time.

Hierarchical configuration – A multi-level CPU configuration that is controlled by a single computer at the top of the multiple CPU hierarchy; the lowest level of the hierarchy is the user level.

I/O control unit – A device that performs code conversion and is located between one or more I/O devices and the CPU; is used only to facilitate I/O operations.

In-house – An organization's use of its own personnel or resources to develop programs or other problem-solving systems.

Input/output bound – A situation in which the CPU is slowed down because of I/O operations which are extremely slow in comparison to CPU internal processing speeds.

Local area networking – An alternate form of distributed processing; involves interconnecting computers in a single building or a complex of buildings.

Local system – Peripherals connected directly to the CPU.

Message-switching – A communications processor with the principal task of receiving messages and routing them to appropriate destinations.

Modem – Also called a data set; a device that modulates and demodulates signals transmitted over communication facilities.

Modulation – A technique used in modems to make data-processing signals compatible with communication facilities.

Multiplexer – A device that permits more than one I/O device to transmit data over the same communication channel.

Multiplexor channel – A limited-capacity computer that can handle more than one I/O device at a time; normally controls slow-speed devices such as card readers, printers, or terminals.

Narrow bandwidth channels – Communication channels that can only transmit data at a rate of forty-five to ninety bits per second; for example, telegraph channels.

Network – The linking together of several CPUs.

Poll – Or polling; the process used by a concentrator to determine if an input/output device wants to send a message to the CPU.

Programmable communications processor – A device that relieves the CPU of the task of monitoring data transmissions.

Pulse form – A pulse of current used to store data in computers.

Remote system – A system in which terminals are connected to the central computer by a communication channel.

Ring configuration – A type of distributed system in which a number of computers are connected by a single transmission line in a ring arrangement.

Selector channel – A channel that can accept input from only one device at a time; usually used with high-speed I/O devices such as a magnetic-tape or magnetic-disk unit.

Simplex – A type of communication channel that provides for unidirectional, or one-way, transmission of data.

Star configuration – A multiple CPU configuration in which all transactions must go through a central computer prior to being routed to the appropriate network computer.

Telecommunication – The combined use of communication facilities, such as telephone systems and data-processing equipment.

Terminals – Input/output devices that are hooked into a communication network.

Time slicing – A technique used in a time-sharing system that allocates a small portion of processing time to each user.

Time-sharing system – A central computer that can be used by various users at the same time for diverse tasks.

Voice-grade channel – A communication channel that has a wider frequency range and can transmit data at a rate of forty-five to ninety bits per second; for example, a telegraph channel.

SUMMARY

Data communication is the electronic transmission of data from one location to another over a communication channel. Combining the use of data-processing equipment with communications facilities, such as telephone systems, is called telecommunication.

Data can be sent by analog transmission (continuous wave form) or by digital transmission (pulse form). In order for communication by computer to occur by analog transmission, the pulses must be converted to waves. This process is called modulation. The conversion back to pulses is called demodulation and occurs at the receiving end before the data is entered into the computers. Modems (from MOdulation and DEModulation), or data sets, accomplish these processes.

Digital transmission does not need the conversion process since computers store data in "on" and "off" or pulse form. Therefore, digital transmission tends to be faster and more accurate than analog transmission.

Input/ouput control units and channels are used in an I/O subsystem to increase the efficiency of the CPU. An I/O control unit converts input data into machine code and vice versa. It also is used in data buffering, the holding of data in temporary areas for transferring to and from the CPU. With a buffer, data can be sent to the CPU in large amounts rather than an item at a time.

Channels also help free the CPU. They are small, limited-capacity computers that serve as data roadways. Channels control I/O operations so that input, output, and processing operations can overlap. Selector channels accept input from one device at a time and are used with high-speed I/O devices. Multiplexor channels can handle more than one I/O device at one time. They are used with low-speed devices. Without channels, the CPU would have to wait for data to be sent to or from an I/O device since I/O devices are much slower than the CPU. When the CPU is slowed because of I/O operations, it is input/output-bound.

Communication channels permit transmission of electrical signals from one location to another. Types of channels include telegraph lines, telephone lines, coaxial cables, microwave links, and communication satellites. Communication channels are classified by the grades of transmission (bandwidth) and the modes of transmission (simplex, half-duplex, full-duplex).

Multiplexers and concentrators increase the number of devices that can use a communication channel, while programmable communication processors relieve the CPU of many tasks it might normally perform in a communication system. Both help a computer system operate more efficiently.

Communication systems can be single or multiple CPU systems. A typical single CPU system consists of a mainframe and peripherals. If the peripherals are connected directly to the CPU, the system is said to be local. Remote systems connected by communication channels are becoming more common.

A time-sharing system allows several users to access the same computer at the same time. Time-sharing can be accomplished in-house or it can be leased from a time-sharing service company. Time-slicing is the concept that permits multiple users to access the same central computer in what seems to be a single-user environment.

In multiple CPU systems, more than one CPU is linked to create a computer network. Configurations for such systems include star, ring, and hierarchical designs. Most networks involve earth-bound telecommunication, but the use of satellite-based networks is growing.

In distributed data processing (DDP), some processing may occur at remote locations before data is sent to the main computer. The amount and type of processing varies from company to company. Managers can use local area networks and electronic mail services as forms of DDP for decision making and communication within an organization.

STRUCTURED LEARNING

1. A modem is a device that
    a. converts data from pulse form to wave form
    b. is often called a data set
    c. converts data from wave form to pulse form
    d. both a and c
    e. all of the above

    *   *   *   *   *   *   *   *   *

    (e) The modem (from MOdulation and DEModulation) takes care of data conversion in the sending and the receiving. It is also called a data set.

2. The I/O control unit is
    a. another name for the control unit of the CPU
    b. a unit that performs data buffering
    c. a unit that performs code conversion
    d. a and c
    e. b and c

    *   *   *   *   *   *   *   *   *

(e) The I/O control unit is a separate unit and is not the same as the control unit of the CPU. It helps with I/O operations, so some of the operations it performs are data buffering and code conversion.

3. Communication channels can be classified by the
   a. transmission mode
   b. width of the frequency band
   c. amount of processing they do
   d. a and b
   e. a and c

   *   *   *   *   *   *   *   *   *

   (d) The width of the frequency band, which is approximately proportional to the quantity of data that can be transmitted, is one way communication channels can be classified. The band widths are narrow, voice-grade and broad-band. Another way of classifying them is by the type of transmission: simplex, half-duplex, and full-duplex. Communication channels do no data processing.

4. A device that receives input from several terminals, combines the input into a stream of data, and then transmits the stream over one communication channel is called a
   a. teletype   c. concentrator
   b. multiplexer   d. modem

   *   *   *   *   *   *   *   *   *

   (b) With a multiplexer, one channel can handle the data transmission that would otherwise be handled by more than one channel. A concentrator polls, or "asks," the devices whether they have something to send, but allows only one to send at a time. A modem only converts data; it does not manage it. A teletype is an I/O device.

5. A front-end processor can perform message-switching and
   a. validation of transmitted data
   b. conversion to pulse form
   c. polling of I/O devices
   d. choosing of band widths

   *   *   *   *   *   *   *   *   *

   (a) The front-end processor can also validate transmitted data. A modem converts data to pulse form and a concentrator polls I/O devices. Band widths are determined by which grade of transmission is desired.

6.   Time-sharing systems have been developed to
      a.   provide computer services for businesses that cannot
            afford to install a computer
      b.   provide an economical alternative for organizations
            that need the power of a large computer system on an
            infrequent basis
      c.   decrease the cost of computers
      d.   both a and b

*   *   *   *   *   *   *   *   *

(d) Many businesses could benefit from the installation of
a computer facility, but feel the cost is prohibitive.
Others may need computer power only on occasion. The time-
sharing concept will help businesses in both situations.

7.   When an organization establishes its own time-sharing fa-
      cility, as opposed to purchasing time-sharing capability
      from a service company, it is said to have a(n)
      a.   resource pooling system   c.   interactive system
      b.   in-house system   d.   hard-wired system

*   *   *   *   *   *   *   *   *

(b) A business can either buy time-sharing from a service
company or establish it within its own organization. When
it is established within its own organization, it is
referred to as an in-house system.

8.   Time-slicing is a way to
      a.   use the resources of a concentrator
      b.   distribute the processing power of the CPU
      c.   purchase computer power
      d.   get the use of a satellite communication system.

*   *   *   *   *   *   *   *   *

(b) Time-slicing is a way for the CPU to process several
programs at once. In doing so, it seems as if each user's
program is being processed at the same time. In reality,
the CPU switches back and forth between several programs at
a rapid rate, so the user believes his or her program is
being processed immediately.

9. A ring configuration can be advantageous because
    a. all transactions go through a central computer before
        being routed to the appropriate network computer
    b. it has single-point vulnerability
    c. it can bypass a malfunctioning unit without disrupting
        other network operations
    d. it is a single CPU configuration

    *   *   *   *   *   *   *   *   *

    (c) A ring configuration is a type of multiple CPU design
    which means it is not dependent on one CPU. Answers a and
    b describe the star configuration.

10. The amount and type of processing that takes place at each
    distributed site in distributed data processing depends on
    a. the structure and management philosophy of the organi-
        zation
    b. whether EFT is used
    c. the decision of the board of directors of a corporation
    d. whether or not the company uses minicomputers

    *   *   *   *   *   *   *   *   *

    (a) A company's managerial philosophy and structure deter-
    mines the type of system and the amount of processing done
    at a distributed site. Some companies may have a strong
    centralized management, while others are more decentral-
    ized.

TRUE/FALSE

1. T F A modem is also called a data set.

2. T F Microwaves can be used for data transfer.

3. T F High-speed I/O devices operate at least as fast as
          the CPU.

4   T F In the simplex mode of transmission, data can be
          transmitted in both directions, but in only one
          direction at a time.

5. T F A multiplexer is used to reduce the speed of a com-
          munication channel.

6.   T F   A programmable communications processor can handle
             some of the tasks of data transmission more effi-
             ciently than the CPU.

7.   T F   In a time-sharing system, the resource pooling that
             takes place actually means higher costs per unit
             than privately owned and maintained applications
             programs and computers.

8.   T F   An advantage to using a hierarchical network is that
             functional departments can meet their processing
             requirements locally but still have access to the
             central facility for jobs that require computing
             power beyond the capabilities of the local computer.

9.   T F   A front-end processor is used to perform message-
             switching functions.

10.   T F   Local area networks provide the interconnecting of
             computers in a single building or complex of
             buildings.

MATCHING

a.	modulation	f.	buffer
b.	input/output bound	f.	communication channel
c.	broad-band	h.	half-duplex
d.	datacom handlers	i.	time-sharing
e.	in-house	j.	star

1.   A channel characterized by high-speed transmission lines,
      such as laser beams, is called a _____ channel.

2.   The link that permits the transmission of electrical
      signals between two distant points is called a(n) _____.

3.   The process of converting data from pulse form to wave form
      is _____.

4.   When time-sharing or other computer functions are developed
      within a firm, it is said to be developed _____.

5.   The network configuration that creates a central decision
      point is the _____ configuration.

6. The system that allows multiple users to access a central computer and believe they are working in a single-user environment is called _____.

7. Multiplexers and concentrators increase the number of devices that can use a communication channel and are known as _____.

8. A temporary holding place for data is a(n) _____.

9. A channel that can transmit information in both directions, but in only one direction at a time is a(n) _____ channel.

10. When a CPU is slowed down by I/O operations, it is said to be _____.

SHORT ANSWERS

1. What is the difference between analog transmission and digital transmission? Which is better and why?

2. How does a buffer increase the efficiency of a computer system?

3.   How do channels increase the efficiency of the CPU?

4.   Why might an analyst choose a full-duplex channel when designing a data communication system?

5.   What channel bandwidth, or grade, is most suitable for applications that required large volumes of data to be transmitted at high speeds?   Name a few examples of this channel grade.

6.   List four advantages of time-sharing.

7.   What is time-slicing?

8.   Explain why an organization might choose a ring con-
      figuration over a star configuration network.

9.   Explain why a company might choose a local area network to
      link computers in a building or complex of buildings.

10.   What problems can you envision for electronic funds
      transfer and automatic teller machine systems? (There is
      no one correct answer.)

ANSWER KEY

True/False

1. T   3. F   5. F   7. F   9. T

Matching

1. c   3. a   5. j   7. d   9. h

Short Answer

1.   Analog transmission sends data in continuous wave form, and
      digital transmission relays data as distinct "on/off"
      pulses. Digital transmission is faster and more accurate
      because it transmits data in the same form that the com-
      puter stores them.

3.   Channels act as data roadways. During processing, the CPU
      tells a channel the input and output needs. The channel
      then goes to the required input device for data or sends
      information to the proper output device. Meanwhile, the
      CPU is free to do other processing.

5.   Broad-band channels are most suitable for high-speed
      transmission of large volumes of data. Examples are
      coaxial cables, microwaves, helical waveguides, and laser
      beams.

7.   Time-slicing is a technique used to allocate computer time
      to a number of users or jobs. Each user is given a small
      portion of processing time. If a user's program is not
      completely executed during this time, for example, the com-
      puter will go on to another job, and later return to the
      original one. The switching of programs occurs at such a
      rapid rate that users are generally unaware of it.

9.   Microcomputers can be linked together, allowing shared
      peripheral devices, such as printers and storage devices,
      and information. In addition, electronic mail is available
      so that members of the network can exchange messages easily
      without unnecessary phone calls and return calls.

SECTION III
PROGRAMMING

8

System
Software

KEY TERMS

Application program – A sequence of instructions written to solve a specific problem facing organizational management.

Back-end processor – A small CPU serving as an interface between a large CPU and a large data base stored on a direct-access storage device.

Background partition – In a multiprogramming system, a partition holding a lower-priority program that is executed only when high-priority programs are not using the system.

Background program – In a multiprogramming system, a program that can be executed whenever the facilities of the system are not needed by a high-priority program.

Batch processing – The grouping of user jobs for processing one after another in a continuous stream--a batch processing environment.

Concurrently – Over the same period of time; in multiprogramming, processing of operations rotates between different programs, giving the illusion of simultaneous (or concurrent) processing.

Control program – A routine, usually part of an operating system, that aids in controlling the operations and management of a computer system.

Foreground partition - Also called foreground area; in a multiprogramming system, a partition containing high-priority application programs.

Foreground program - In a multiprogramming system, a program that has high priority.

Front-end processor - A small CPU serving as an interface between a large CPU and peripheral devices.

Input/output management system - A subsystem of the operating system that controls and coordinates the CPU while receiving input from channels, executing instructions of programs in storage, and regulating output.

Interrupt - A control signal from a sensor-band input or output unit that requests the extension of the control unit of the CPU from the current operation.

Job-control language (JCL) - A language that serves as the communication link between the programmer and the operating system.

Job-control program - A control program that translates the job-control statements written by a programmer into machine-language instructions that can be executed by the computer.

Language-translator program - Software that translates the English-like programs written by programmers into machine-executable code.

Librarian program - Software that manages the storage and use of library programs by maintaining a directory of programs in the system library and appropriate procedures for additions and deletions.

Library programs - User-written or manufacturer-supplied programs and subroutines that are frequently used in other programs; they are written and stored on secondary storage and called into primary storage when needed.

Linkage editor - A subprogram of the operating system that links the object program from the system residence device to primary storage.

Memory management - In a multi-programming environment, the process of keeping the programs in primary storage separate.

Memory protection - See Memory management.

Multiprocessing – A multiple CPU configuration in which jobs are processed simultaneously.

Multiprogramming – A technique whereby several programs are placed in primary storage at the same time, giving the illusion that they are being executed simultaneously; this results in increased CPU active time.

Object program – A sequence of machine-executable instructions derived from source-program statements by a language translator program.

Online – In direct communication with the computer.

Operating system – A collection of programs designed to permit a computer system to manage itself and to avoid idle CPU time while increasing utilization of computer resources.

Overlapped processing – A method of processing where the computer works on several programs instead of one.

Page frame – In a virtual-storage environment, one of the fixed-size physical areas into which primary storage is divided.

Page – In a virtual-storage environment, the portion of a program that is kept in secondary storage and loaded into real storage only when needed during processing.

Paging – A method of implementing virtual storage; data and programs are broken into fixed-size blocks, or pages, and loaded into real storage when needed during processing.

Partition – In multiprogramming, the primary storage area reserved for one program; may be fixed or variable in size; see also Region.

Processing program – A routine, usually part of the operating system, that is used to simplify program preparation and execution.

Real storage – See Primary storage; contrast with virtual storage.

Region – In multiprogramming with a variable number of tasks, a term often used to mean the internal space allocated; a variable-size partition.

Resident routines – The most frequently used components of the supervisor which are initially loaded into primary storage.

Segmentation – A method of implementing virtual storage; involves dividing a program into variable-size blocks, called segments, depending on the program logic.

Segment – A variable-size block or portion of a program used in a virtual storage system.

Serial processing – A method of processing where programs are executed one at a time, usually found in simple operating systems such as the earliest computer systems.

Sort/merge programs – A part of the operating-system utility programs; used to sort records to facilitate updating and subsequent combining of files to form a single, updated file.

Source program – A sequence of instructions written in either assembly language or high-level language that is translated into an object program.

Subroutine – A sequence of statements not within the main line of the program; saves the programmer time by not having to write the same instructions over again in different parts of the program.

Supervisor program – Also known as a monitor or executive; the major component of the operating system; coordinates the activities of all other parts of the operating system.

Swapping – In a virtual-storage environment, the process of transferring a program section from virtual storage to real storage, and vice versa.

System library – A collection of files in which various parts of an operating system are stored.

System program – A sequence of instructions written to coordinate the operation of all computer circuitry and to help the computer run quickly and efficiently.

System residence device – An auxiliary storage device (disk, tape, or drum) on which operating-system programs are stored and from which they are loaded into primary storage.

Thrashing – Programs in which little actual processing occurs in comparison to the amount of swapping done.

Transient routine – A supervisor routine that remains in primary storage with the remainder of the operating system.

Utility **program** – A program within an operating system that performs a specialized function.

Virtual memory – See Virtual storage.

Virtual storage – An extension of multiprogramming in which portions of programs not being used are kept in secondary storage until needed, giving the impression that primary storage is unlimited; contrast with real storage.

SUMMARY

The computer must be told what to do by a series of instructions called a program. The two basic types of programs are system programs and application programs.

System programs control the operations of the computer; they are tailored to a particular computer and cannot be used on other computers without extensive modification. Application programs are designed to solve the particular information needs of an organization such as accounting and inventory control. Application programs are written in high-level languages and can be used on different computers with minor modification. Language-translator programs convert the English-like programs written by programmers into machine language.

The operating system, a collection of system programs, enables the computer to manage its own operations. It is responsible for scheduling and prioritizing jobs, allocating computer resources such as CPU time and I/O devices, and resolving conflicts. The two types of operating systems are batch and online.

A batch operating system groups several user programs together to be processed in a continuous stream. An online operating system can respond to spontaneous requests for system resources.

The operating system actually consists of two types of programs: control programs and processing programs. Control programs oversee system operations and perform tasks such as input/output, scheduling, handling interrupts, and communicating with the computer operator. Processing programs are executed under the supervision of control programs and are used to simplify the preparation of programs.

The most important control program is the supervisor program which coordinates the activities of all other parts of the operating system. The job-control program translates the job-control statements written by a programmer into machine-language instructions. The input/output management system oversees and coordinates the movement of input from channels to the CPU, the execution of instructions or programs in storage, and the regulation of output.

The main processing programs are the language-translators, linkage editor, library programs, and utility programs.

The first computer systems executed programs using serial processing (executing one program at a time) which left the high-speed CPU idle for long periods. Multiprogramming increases CPU active time by processing several programs concurrently. While I/O operations from one program are being performed, the CPU can execute instructions from other programs.

An extension of multiprogramming, virtual storage, saves space in primary storage by keeping only the portion of the program immediately needed in primary storage. Therefore, more programs can reside in primary storage at the same time to be executed upon. Virtual storage gives the illusion of unlimited primary storage by moving portions of programs back and forth between real storage (primary storage within the CPU) and virtual storage (direct-access storage). This process is known as swapping.

Another method to improve CPU efficiency is to link several CPUs together for coordinated operation. This is called multiprocessing and it allows for several program instructions to be executed simultaneously by different CPUs. Several large CPUs can be linked together to handle extremely large, complex data-processing needs. Or a large CPU can be linked to small CPUs which can then handle tasks such as scheduling, editing data, and maintaining files.

STRUCTURED LEARNING

1.   Programs used in inventory control, accounting, or any specific data-processing task are called
     a.   processing programs   c.   application programs
     b.   system programs   d.   utility programs

     *   *   *   *   *   *   *   *   *

(c) Application programs solve an organization's information needs. Processing, system, and utility programs perform specfic functions for the operating system.

2.   An operating system that can respond to spontaneous requests for system resources is
    a.   a batch operating system
    b.   a stacked-job operating system
    c.   an immediate response (IR) operating system
    d.   an online operating system

    *   *   *   *   *   *   *   *   *

    (d) An online operating system is one that can respond to spontaneous requests for system resources, such as management inquiries entered from online terminals.

3.   Control programs oversee system operations and perform tasks such as
    a.   input/output and scheduling
    b.   handling interrupts
    c.   simplifying program preparation
    d.   handling communication with the computer operator or programmer
    e.   a, b, and c
    f.   a, b, and d

    *   *   *   *   *   *   *   *   *

    (f) Processing programs are used to simplify program preparation and are executed by control programs.

4.   The major component of the operating system is
    a.   the I/O management system
    b.   the library program
    c.   the supervisor program
    d.   the compiler

    *   *   *   *   *   *   *   *   *

    (c) The supervisor program (also called the monitor or executive) coordinates the activities of all other parts of the operating system. It is needed at all times and remains in primary storage throughout processing.

5.   The job-control program
      a.   is a processing program
      b.   translates the job-control statements written by a
           programmer into machine-language instructions
      c.   moves data between I/O devices and specific memory
           locations
      d.   both a and b

      *   *   *   *   *   *   *   *   *

      (b) The job-control program is a control program that
      translates programmer-written, job-control statements into
      instructions that can be executed by the computer. It is
      called into primary storage by the supervisor only when it
      is needed to translate a job-control statement.

6.   During multiprogramming, programs that are in primary
      storage are kept separate by using
      a.   inter-gap blocks   c.   regions
      b.   memory modules   d.   bundles

      *   *   *   *   *   *   *   *   *

      (c) Regions (or partitions) are areas in primary memory for
      programs--each partition is reserved for one program.

7.   Limitations to virtual storage include
      a.   the need to assign priorities to programs
      b.   the need for large amounts of internal storage
      c.   an inefficient use of primary storage space
      d.   setting partitions large enough to hold an entire
           program

      *   *   *   *   *   *   *   *   *

      (b) Virtual storage requires large amounts of internal
      storage. Answers a, c, and d are all limitations to
      multiprogramming.

8.   Virtual storage
     a.   gives the illusion that primary storage is unlimited
     b.   loads the highest priority programs into foreground
          partitions
     c.   makes it possible for more programs to be executed
          within a given time period since portions of several
          programs can be resident in primary storage simulta-
          neously
     d.   both a and c

     *   *   *   *   *   *   *   *   *

     (d) In virtual storage (virtual memory), only the portion
     of a program that is needed immediately is in primary
     storage at any given time; the rest of the program and data
     can be kept in secondary storage. Thus, the size limita-
     tion of primary storage is minimized. Foreground par-
     titions are used in multiprogramming.

9.   The method of implementing virtual storage in which primary
     storage is divided into fixed-size physical areas is called
     a.   paging   c.   partitioning
     b.   segmentation   d.   framing

     *   *   *   *   *   *   *   *   *

     (a) Paging divides primary storage into fixed-size physical
     areas called page frames. All page frames for all programs
     are the same size.

10. Which is true of multiprocessing?
     a.   Two or more CPUs are linked together for coordinated
          operation.
     b.   The computer appears to be processing different jobs
          simultaneously although this is not really the case.
     c.   A large CPU handles scheduling, data editing, and file
          maintenance tasks and a smaller one handles the large
          mathematical calculations.
     d.   none of the above

     *   *   *   *   *   *   *   *   *

     (a) Multiprocessing involves the use of two or more central
     processing units linked together for coordinated operation.
     The configuration can have small CPUs linked to large CPUs
     or two or more large CPUs linked together.

TRUE/FALSE

1.   T F   When a computer operator groups all user programs together for processing, it is called batch processing.

2.   T F   System programs are written for a particular computer but can be easily executed on other computers.

3.   T F   Operating systems are usually stored on a secondary storage device known as the system residence device.

4.   T F   Programs that transfer data from file to file or from one I/O device to another are utility programs.

5   T F   The sequence of instructions written in high-level language is called an object program.

6.   T F   Under multiprogramming, programs of the lowest priority are loaded into background partitions and are called background programs.

7.   T F   The communication link between programmers and the operating system is the job-control language.

8.   T F   Real storage usually refers to primary storage within the CPU, while virtual storage refers to direct-access storage.

9.   T F   Before the application program is translated into machine language by the appropriate language translator, it is called the object program.

10.   T F   When the CPU executes various programs concurrently, it is the same as processing them simultaneously.

MATCHING

       a.   foreground   f.   real
       b.   paging   g.   monitor
       c.   back-end processor   h.   segmentation
       d.   serial   i.   thrashing
       e.   region   j.   front-end processor

1.   Under multiprogramming, the highest priority programs are called _____ programs.

2.   A method of implementing virtual storage that breaks
     programs into logical units is called _____.

3.   An operating system that can work on only one program at a
     time uses _____ processing.

4.   _____ is another name for the supervisor program.

5.   An interface between the CPU and online terminals is called
     a(n) _____.

6.   _____ occurs during virtual storage when much time is
     spent locating and exchanging program segments compared to
     the actual time spent processing.

7.   _____ is a method of implementing virtual storage which
     breaks programs into fixed-sized units.

8.   Primary storage within the CPU is often called _____
     storage.

9.   An interface between the CPU and a large data base stored
     on direct-access storage devices is called a(n) _____.

10. A variable-sized area used in multiprogramming to hold a
     program is known as a(n) _____.

SHORT ANSWER

1.   What are the major processing programs contained in the
     operating system? What purposes do they serve?

2.   How does a computer's operating system achieve maximum
     efficiency in its processing operations.

3.   What are utility programs used for?   Give examples of some
     utility programs.

4.   What is the difference between library programs and
     librarian programs?   Explain.

5.   What is the purpose of job-control statements?

6. How does multiprogramming increase system efficiency?

7. What is serial processing and why is it inefficient?

8. What are the major limitations of virtual storage?

9. Why can't system programs be easily transferred to other computers?

10.   What is a front-end processor and what purpose does it
       serve? What is a back-end processor and what purpose does
       it serve?

ANSWER KEY

True/False

1. T   3. T   5. F   7. T   9. F

Matching

1. a   3. d   5. j   7. b   . 9. c

Short Answer

1.   The major processing programs are language translators,
      linkage editor, library programs, and utility programs.
      These programs facilitate efficient processing operations
      by simplifying the preparation and execution of programs
      for users.

3.   Utility programs perform specialized functions such as
      transferring data from file to file, or from one I/O device
      to another. Sort/merge programs are used to sort records
      into a certain sequence to help in the updating of files.

5.   Job-control statements are used to specify the beginning of
      a program, to identify the program to be executed, to
      describe the work to be done, and to indicate the I/O de-
      vices to be used.

7.   Early computer systems executed programs using serial proc-
      essing which means that only one program can be executed at
      a time. Serial processing is inefficient because the CPU
      is much faster than I/O devices and it remains idle for
      long periods while I/O operations are being performed.

9.   System programs are written in machine language which is
      very specific for each particular computer. In order to be
      used on another computer, the programs would have to be
      greatly modified.

Programming and Software Development

KEY TERMS

Accumulator – A register that accumulates results of computations.

American National Standards Institute (ANSI) – The institute that adopted a standard set of flowchart symbols which are commonly accepted and used by programmers.

Assembler program – The translator program for an assembly language program; produced a machine language program (object program).

Assembly language – A symbolic programming language that uses convenient abbreviations rather than groupings of 0s and 1s; intermediate-level language in terms of user orientation.

Block diagram – See Flowchart.

Branch – A statement used to bypass or alter the normal flow of execution.

Compiler program – The translator program for high-level languages such as FORTRAN or COBOL; translates source-program statements into machine-executable code.

Counter – A method of controlling a loop in which a specific value is entered into the program and that value is tested each time the loop is executed; when the proper value is reached, the loop can be terminated.

Debugging – The process of locating, isolating, and resolving errors within a program.

Desk-checking – A method used in both system and application program debugging in which the sequence of operations is mentally traced to verify the correctness of the processing logic.

Desk-debugging – See Desk-checking.

Detail flowchart – Depicts the processing steps required within a particular program.

Dump program – A printout that lists the contents of registers and primary-storage locations.

Flowchart – Of two kinds: the program flowchart, which is a graphic representation of the types and sequences of operations in a program; and the system flowchart, which shows the flow of data through an entire system.

Flowlines – The lines that connect flowchart symbols.

High-level languages – English-like coding schemes that are procedure-, problem-, and user-oriented.

Interpreter – A high-level language translator that evaluates and translates a program one statement at a time; used extensively on microcomputer systems because it takes less primary storage than a compiler.

Interpreter program – See Interpreter.

Language-translator program – Software that translates the English-like programs written by programmers into machine-executable code.

Logic diagram – See Flowchart.

Loop – A series of instructions that are executed repeatedly as long as specified conditions remain constant.

Machine language – The only set of instructions that a computer can execute directly; a code that designates the proper electrical states in the computer as combinations of 0s and 1s.

Macro flowchart – See Modular program flowchart.

Micro flowchart – See Detail flowchart.

Mnemonics – A symbolic name (memory aid); used in symbolic languages (for example, assembly language) and high-level programming languages.

Modular program flowchart – A diagram that represents the general flow and major processing steps (modules) of a program.

Module – A part of a whole; a program segment; a subsystem.

Object program – A sequence of machine-executable instructions derived from source-program statements by a language translator program.

Pseudocode – An informal design language used to represent the logic patterns of structured programming.

Run book – Also known as the operator's manual; program documentation designed to aid the computer operator in running a program.

Selection – Program logic that includes a test; depending on the results of the test, one of two paths is taken.

Simple sequence – Program logic where one statement after another is executed in order, as stored.

Source program – A sequence of instructions written in either assembly language or high-level language that is translated into an object program.

Syntax – Refers to the way rules must be followed while coding instructions, just as grammatical rules must be followed in English.

Systems analyst – The person who is the communication link or interface between users and technical persons (such as computer programmers and operators); responsible for system analysis, design, and implementation of computer-based information systems.

Trace – Hard-copy list of the steps followed during program execution in the order they occurred.

Trace program – A program that is used for a trace.

Trailer value – A method of controlling a loop in which a unique item signals the computer to stop performing the loop.

SUMMARY

Computers have no intelligence of their own.   Therefore, the programmer must instruct the computer in every step necessary to solve a given problem.   In order to do this, the programmer needs to have an organized method of problem-solving. The problem-solving process may be broken down into these five steps:

- Defining the problem.
- Designing a solution.
- Writing the program.
- Compiling, debugging, and testing the program.
- Documenting the program.

Defining the problem involves determining what output the program is to obtain.   Then it is possible to determine the needed input and what processing will have to be done.

Designing a solution requires an understanding of the four basic logic patterns computers use: simple sequence, selection, loop, and branch.   When statements are executed in the same order in which they occur in a program, this is simple sequence. Selection is involved when a comparison is made.   A loop allows a section of a program to be repeated as many times as needed. A branch statement allows the programmer to skip (or branch) to a desired program statement.   It is often difficult to follow the logic of programs with numerous branches.

Pseudocode and flowcharting are techniques that help programmers solve programming problems.   Pseudocode involves writing a narrative description of the processing steps a program will need to include.   This is done using English-like statements.   Flowcharts visually represent the logic of a program.   Modular program flowcharts (also called macro flowcharts) outline the general flow and major segments of a program.   Detail, or micro, flowcharts list all the processing steps that will be necessary in the final program.

Accumulators are used in loops to keep track of the totals of specified items.   The final value of the accumulator is usually printed outside the loop.

When actually writing a program, the programmer uses a programming language.   High-level languages consist of comments, declarations, input/output statements, computations, and transfers of control.

Well-written programs will have these characteristics:

- They will be easy to read and understand.
- They will be efficient.
- They will be reliable, consistently producing correct output.
- They will be robust, that is they will work under all conditions.
- They will be easy to update and modify.

The three levels of programming languages are: machine language, assembly language, and high-level languages. Computers are only able to directly execute programs that are in machine language. Machine language consists of combinations of 0s and 1s. Assembly language is one step above machine language. High-level languages, such as FORTRAN, are more English-like, and therefore are easier for people to understand.

Assembly and high-level languages must be converted to machine language by a language-translator program.

Debugging refers to the process of finding errors in a program and correcting them. Testing involves running a program using input that represents the data the program will actually use. Care should be taken to determine that the program will work for all types of data.

Programmers use many debugging methods. Desk-debugging is when the programmer pretends to be the computer and goes through a program in the same way the computer would. A dump program lists the contents of the registers and primary storage which can often help determine what is wrong with a program. A trace lists all of the steps a program goes through during execution and will often pinpoint where errors are occurring.

Properly documenting a program is very important. Maintaining and modifying a program is much easier if the program is well-documented.

STRUCTURED LEARNING

1.   Which of the following is not included as part of defining
     the problem?
     a.   determine the needed input
     b.   write the pseudocode for the program
     c.   state the solution in terms of clear, concise objec-
          tives
     d.   determine what processing will be needed

     *   *   *   *   *   *   *   *   *

     (b) Writing the pseudocode for a program is done after
     defining the problem. It is part of designing a solution.
     Determining the needed input, stating the solution in terms
     of clear, concise objectives, and determining what proc-
     essing will be needed are all parts of defining the
     problem.

2.   A selection pattern requires the computer to
     a.   repeat a section of the program
     b.   branch to another part of the program
     c.   continue on with the next statement
     d.   make a comparison

     *   *   *   *   *   *   *   *   *

     (d) When executing a selection pattern, the computer will
     always have to make a comparison. It does this by com-
     paring the contents of one memory location with another.
     The computer can only determine if the two values are equal
     or if one is greater than or less than the other.

3.   Which one of the following languages would a source program
     never be written in?
     a.   assembly language   c.   machine language
     b.   a high-level language   d.   FORTRAN

     *   *   *   *   *   *   *   *   *

     (c) A source program will never be written in machine code
     because a source program is a program that needs to be
     translated before it can be executed. Machine code
     programs can be executed directly by the computer.
     Assembly, high-level, and FORTRAN (which is a high-level
     language) must always be translated first.

4.   When a program is translated into machine language, the
       result is referred to as
       a.   the object program   c.   the assembler
       b.   the source program   d.   a high-level language

       *   *   *   *   *   *   *   *   *

       (a) When a program is translated into machine code, the
       result of this process is referred to as the object
       program. The source program is the one being translated.

5.   A program which always gets correct results is
       demonstrating
       a.   reliability   c.   efficiency
       b.   robustness   d.   ease of maintenance

       *   *   *   *   *   *   *   *   *

       (a) A program which consistently, over a period of many
       executions, continues to obtain correct results is said to
       be reliable. Robustness, on the other hand, refers to the
       ability of the program to keep working, regardless of the
       conditions under which it is working.

6.   The flowchart symbol   ☐   indicates
       a.   a start or stop step   c.   a processing step
       b.   a decision step   d.   an input/output step

       *   *   *   *   *   *   *   *   *

       (c) The symbol   ☐   indicates a processing step, such as
       adding numbers together, or doing other kinds of com-
       putations.

7.   The   ⬭   symbol in a flowchart is used to represent a(n)
       a.   start or stop step   c.   processing step
       b.   decision step   d.   input/output step

       *   *   *   *   *   *   *   *   *

       (a) The symbol   ⬭   is always used at the beginning and
       the end of a program flowchart.

8.   The purpose of an accumulator is to
     a.   keep track of totals of certain items
     b.   make a comparison
     c.   branch to a desired section of the program
     d.   read numbers

     *   *   *   *   *   *   *   *   *

     (a) Accumulators are used to keep track of totals of cer-
     tain items. For example, if the programmer wanted to read
     20 numbers and print their total, a loop would be used to
     read the numbers. Each time a number was read, this new
     value would be added to the accumulator. After all the
     numbers were read, the value of the accumulator could be
     printed outside the loop.

9.   Comments
     a.   declare variables to be used in the program
     b.   read data for use by the program
     c.   are ignored by the computer
     d.   are useful only to the computer

     *   *   *   *   *   *   *   *   *

     (c) Comments mean nothing to the computer and are simply
     ignored by it. They are there to explain the program to
     people. People who use this documentation include program-
     mers, computer operators, and management personnel.

10. An interpreter is a language-translator program which
     a.   translates assembly language to machine language
     b.   translates the entire source program before executing
          it
     c.   is not used with microcomputers
     d.   translates and executes a program one statement at a
          time

     *   *   *   *   *   *   *   *   *

     (d) An interpreter is a language translator which trans-
     lates and executes a program one statement at a time. This
     is unlike compilers and assemblers which translate the
     entire program before execution. Interpreters are usually
     smaller than assemblers or compilers and therefore have
     been widely used on microcomputers.

TRUE/FALSE

1. T F   The first step in the problem-solving process is designing a solution.

2. T F   The solution to a problem should be stated in terms of clear, concise objectives.

3. T F   Before the needed input can be determined, it is necessary to define what output is desired.

4. T F   Computers use only four basic logic patterns.

5. T F   In a simple sequence pattern, the computer must make a comparison.

6. T F   A trailer value tells the computer that there are no more data to be input.

7. T F   Using many branches in a program makes the logic of the program easy to follow.

8. T F   In order to write pseudocode, a person must know a programming language.

9. T F   A flowchart which shows only how the major parts of a program work together is referred to as a detail flowchart.

10. T F   A compiler translates and executes a program one statement at a time.

MATCHING

a. machine language
b. output
c. reliable
d. source
e. pseudocode

f. system analyst
g. debugging
h. dump program
i. comments
j. flowchart

1. A(n) _____ often defines and designs a solution to a problem, but does not actually write the program.

2. The results obtained by a program after it has been executed are the program _____.

3.   _____ consists of English-like statements giving all the steps necessary in a program.

4.   A(n) _____ visually represents the logic of a program.

5.   Remarks in a program used to explain program segments to people are called _____.

6.   The only language a computer can directly execute is _____.

7.   The _____ program is what the programmer writes.

8.   The process of locating and fixing program errors is called _____.

9.   A(n) _____ gives the contents of registers and primary storage.

10. Programs that are _____ consistently produce the correct results.

SHORT ANSWER

1.   Explain what is meant by defining the problem.

2.   List the four basic logic patterns used by computers.

3.   Why are loops important in programming?

4.   What is the difference between a macro and a micro
      flowchart?

5.   List at least three desirable qualities of a well-written
      program.

6.   What does it mean to say that a program is robust?

7.   Explain the difference between a flowchart and pseudocode.

8.   Name two methods of controlling a loop.   Give a brief
     description of each.

9.   What is the purpose of a language-translator program?

10. What is the purpose of a trace program?   How does it help
     the programmer?

ANSWER KEY

True/False

1. F   3. T   5. F   7. F   9. F

Matching

1. f   3. e   5. i   7. d   9. h

Short Answer

1. When defining the problem, first the solution must be stated in clear, concise terms. Then it can be determined what input will be needed to obtain this solution. Finally, any processing that will need to be done can be stated.

3. Loops allow a particular section of a program to be repeated as many times as necessary. This allows the computer to perform the same task over and over. Computers are ideally suited to repetitious jobs.

5. A well-written program should have the following qualities:

    - It should be easy to read and understand.
    - It should be efficient.
    - It should be reliable, consistently producing correct output.
    - It should be robust, that is, it should work under all conditions.
    - It should be easy to maintain.

7. A flowchart is a visual representation of the logic of a program. Pseudocode is a series of English-like statements listing the steps of a program. Since the flowchart simply outlines program logic, it does not necessarily list every step of a program.

9. The purpose of a language-translator program is to translate an assembly language or a high-level language program into machine language.

Programming Languages

KEY TERMS

Ada – A high-level programming language developed for use by the Department of Defense. Named for Ada Augusta Byron, Countess of Lovelace and daughter of Lord Byron, the poet.

Alphanumeric – A character set that contains letters, digits, and special characters such as punctuation marks.

APL (A Programming Language) – A terminal-oriented, symbolic programming language especially suitable for interactive problem-solving.

Arrays – An ordered set of data items; also called a table or matrix.

Array variable – A symbol that can be used to represent groups of similar data items.

Assembly language – A symbolic programming language that uses convenient abbreviations rather than groupings of 0s and 1s; intermediate-level language in terms of user orientation.

BASIC (Beginners' All-Purpose Symbolic Instruction Code) – A programming language commonly used for interactive problem solving by users who may not be professional programmers.

Built-in functions – Common or often-used procedures that are permanently stored in the computer; examples include square root, absolute value, and logarithmic functions.

COBOL (COmmon Business Oriented Language) – A high-level programming language generally used for accounting and business data processing.

CODASYL (COnference on DAta SYstems Languages) – A committee formed by the Department of Defense to examine the feasibility of establishing a common business programming language.

Default – A course of action chosen by the compiler when several alternatives exist but none have been stated explicitly by the programmer.

Definition mode – When APL is used in this mode, a series of instructions is entered into memory, and the entire program is executed on command from the programmer.

Execution mode – When APL is used in this mode, the terminal can be used much like a desk calculator.

FORTRAN (FORmula TRANslator) – A programming language used primarily in performing mathematical or scientific operations.

Input/output-bound – A situation in which the CPU is slowed down because of I/O operations which are extremely slow in comparison to CPU internal processing speeds.

Label – A name written beside an instruction that acts as a key or identifier for it.

Logo – An education-oriented, procedure-oriented, interactive programming language designed to allow anyone to begin to program and communicate with computers.

Machine Language – The only set of instructions that a computer can execute directly; a code that designates the proper electrical states in the computer as combinations of 0s and 1s.

Mnemonics – A symbolic name (memory aid); used in symbolic languages (for example, assembly language) and high-level programming languages.

Natural languages – Designed primarily for novice computer users; use English-like sentences usually for the purpose of accessing data in a data base.

Op code – Short for operation code; the part of an instruction that tells what operation is to be performed.

Operand - The part of an instruction that tells where to find the data to be operated on.

Pascal - Named after French mathematician Blaise Pascal; an example of a language developed for educational purposes, to teach programming concepts to students.

PL/I (Programming Language One) - A general-purpose programming language used for both scientific and business applications.

Process-bound - A condition that occurs whan a program monopolizes the processing facilities of the computer, making it impossible for other programs to be executed.

Query languages - See Natural languages.

Queue - A list, or collection of programs waiting for execution by the CPU; normally ordered on a first-in, first-out basis.

RPG (Report Program Generator) - An example of a problem-oriented language originally designed to produce business reports.

Simple variable - A variable within the FORTRAN programming language that stands for a single data item.

Single variable - See Simple variable.

Subscript - The integer enclosed within parentheses that allows reference to a specific element.

Turtle - A triangular object used in the Logo programming language to allow users to program graphics interactively.

SUMMARY

Batch programming is often used when the results of a program are not needed immediately. These programs are placed in a queue and executed when the CPU is ready for them. Frequently, these programs are executed at times when computer demand is low, such as at night. Conversely, interactive programming allows the programmer or user to communicate directly with the computer.

Machine language and assembly language are both machine-oriented programming languages. They make efficient use of CPU time but are difficult and tedious to use when writing programs.

High-level languages may be divided into two groups: those that are procedure-oriented and those that are problem-oriented. Procedure-oriented languages require the programmer to describe all the computational and logical procedures needed by the program. In problem-oriented languages, only the problem and the solution need to be described.

Some high-level languages are most appropriate for scientific purposes while others were designed for business applications. The following are examples of high-level languages:

● FORTRAN, the first high-level language developed, is excellent for dealing with mathematical applications. But it does not process alphabetic data or files efficiently.

● APL is a good example of an interactive programming language. In the execution mode, the terminal behaves like a calculator. In the definition mode, instructions can be stored in memory and the entire program can be executed when needed.

● COBOL, the most common business language, was developed to be machine-independent. This means that, in general, COBOL programs can be run on any computer. COBOL programs must have four divisions: IDENTIFICATION, ENVIRONMENT, DATA, and PROCEDURE. COBOL programs are largely self-documenting and are excellent when dealing with large files. COBOL programs tend to be wordy and can quickly become very lengthy.

● RPG was originally designed to produce business reports. Since it is a problem-oriented language, little programming skill is required to write programs in RPG.

● Ada was developed for use by the Department of Defense. It is derived from Pascal and may one day replace COBOL as the most commonly used programming language.

● BASIC is the programming language most widely used on microcomputers. It is easy to learn and requires no programming experience. There are many different versions of BASIC which can lead to problems in transferring programs from one computer to another.

● Logo allows children to learn to program quickly. It is simple and has excellent interactive graphics. It encourages programs to be broken down into smaller procedures.

● PL/I is an all-purpose language that combines the best features of COBOL and FORTRAN. It contains default features and built-in functions.

● Pascal was originally developed to teach programming concepts to students, but its use has expanded to include business and scientific applications. It is a structured language that is relatively easy to learn.

Natural, or query, languages allow users to ask questions using English-like statements. They generally access information contained in data bases.

Program applications are said to be input/output-bound if they need to handle large files. They are said to be process-bound if they require a great many computations.

The programming language chosen for a particular application will depend on the results needed and the type of processing and input/output handling to be done. Then the language best suited for these needs can be determined.

STRUCTURED LEARNING

1. In machine language and assembly language programming, op codes
    a. tell the computer where to find needed data
    b. are not specific to a particular computer
    c. tell the computer what function to perform
    d. are used to document a program

    *   *   *   *   *   *   *   *   *   *

    (c) Op codes are used in machine language to tell the computer what functions to perform. They are not standardized and therefore vary depending on the type of computer being used. The operand tells the computer where to find the data to use when performing the function.

2.   Which of the following is not an advantage of assembly
      language programming?
      a.   It makes efficient use of storage space.
      b.   It makes efficient use of computer time.
      c.   It is easy to write.
      d.   It encourages modular programming.

      *   *   *   *   *   *   *   *   *   *

      (c)   While assembly language programs use storage space and
      computer time efficiently, they are not easy to write.   In
      fact, they are tedious and require a high degree of
      attention to detail.   The assembly language programmer
      needs to have a great deal of programming skill.

3.   The language supported most often by microcomputers is
      a.   APL   c.   BASIC
      b.   COBOL   d.   FORTRAN

      *   *   *   *   *   *   *   *   *   *

      (c)   BASIC interpreters are often built into
      microcomputers.   This is because BASIC programming is easy
      for the novice to learn and BASIC interpreters do not
      require as much storage space as compilers for other
      high-level languages such as FORTRAN, COBOL, and APL.
      Also, BASIC is useful for a wide variety of applications.

4.   The PROCEDURE DIVISION in a COBOL program
      a.   gives program documentation
      b.   is machine-dependent
      c.   describes variables, records, and files used by the
           program
      d.   is where processing is done

      *   *   *   *   *   *   *   *   *   *

      (d)   The PROCEDURE DIVISION is where data are processed.
      Program documentation is given in the IDENTIFICATION
      DIVISION.   The PROCEDURE DIVISION does not change from one
      computer to another when the program is executed.
      Variables, records, and files are described in the DATA
      DIVISION so that they may be used in the PROCEDURE
      DIVISION.

5.   A major disadvantage of BASIC is
     a.   BASIC programs may need to be modified when they are
          moved from one system to another.
     b.   It is difficult to learn.
     c.   It is basically useful only for mathematical
          computations.
     d.   BASIC statements tend to be long and difficult to
          understand.

     *   *   *   *   *   *   *   *   *   *

     (a)   Although BASIC is easy to learn and understand and
     useful for many applications, it is not well standardized.
     Therefore, BASIC programs may need substantial modification
     before they can be run on a system different from the one
     for which they were originally written.

6.   Pascal was originally written
     a.   to be used for business applications
     b.   to teach programming concepts
     c.   to do complex mathematical computations
     d.   to handle large files

     *   *   *   *   *   *   *   *   *   *

     (b)   Niklaus Wirth wrote Pascal to teach programming
     concepts to students.   Therefore, it is a simple, easy to
     learn programming language.   Wirth particularly wanted to
     stress the importance of structured programming, so Pascal
     is a highly structured language, discouraging the use of
     GOTO statements.

7.   Query languages
     a.   are easy for the novice to learn
     b.   have excellent graphics capabilities
     c.   are close to machine language
     d.   use statements similar to assembly language

     *   *   *   *   *   *   *   *   *   *

     (a)   Query languages are very high-level languages that
     require no programming experience and are very easy to use.
     The user enters an English-like question to the computer.
     Generally, the computer obtains the answer by searching a
     data base.

8. A programming application that is process-bound will
    a. require a great many computations
    b. require large files to be processed
    c. be most appropriately written in an education-oriented
        language such as BASIC or Pascal
    d. be easiest to write in a problem-oriented language

    *   *   *   *   *   *   *   *   *   *

    (a) An application that is process-bound is one that
    requires a great deal of mathematical computation, and will
    be best written in a language such as FORTRAN, which was
    developed specifically for this purpose.

9. Which of the following languages would be appropriate for a
    programming application that is heavily input/output-
    bound?
    a. FORTRAN   c. Pascal
    b. BASIC   d. COBOL

    *   *   *   *   *   *   *   *   *   *

    (d) COBOl would be the most appropriate choice since it
    has the abilty to deal with large files efficiently. This
    is not true of the other three choices.

10. The use of high-level languages in computer programming is
    a. decreasing
    b. increasing
    c. remaining about the same
    d. becoming more expensive as compared to using low-level
        languages

    *   *   *   *   *   *   *   *   *   *

    (b) The use of high-level languages is increasing because
    of their ease of use and the decreasing cost of computer
    hardware. Since the cost of programmers' time is always
    increasing, it is important that languages are used that
    make efficient use of this time.

TRUE/FALSE

1.   T   F   Batch programs are executed immediately after being submitted to the computer.

2.   T   F   The earliest computers were programmed in machine language.

3.   T   F   Programs written in assembly language are more efficient than those written in high-level languages.

4.   T   F   FORTRAN is the oldest high-level language.

5.   T   F   Arrays are used to handle simple variables.

6.   T   F   COBOL is often used to evaluate mathematical formulas.

7.   T   F   Ada is a high-level language that was derived from Pascal.

8.   T   F   Logo is a complex high-level language that is difficult to learn.

9.   T   F   Pascal is not a structured programming language.

10. T   F   Query languages are similar to assembly language.

MATCHING

a.   mnemonics
b.   APL
c.   RPG
d.   BASIC
e.   Ada

f.   COBOL
g.   queue
h.   procedure-oriented languages
i.   interactive programming
j.   Logo

1.   _____ allows the programmer to communicate directly with the computer.

2.   Symbolic names used to specify machine operations are called _____.

3.   _____ place an emphasis on computational and logical procedures.

4. _____ may be used in either execution mode or definition mode.

5. The most frequently used business programming language is _____

6. _____ was developed for use by the Department of Defense.

7. The programming language _____ has well-designed interactive graphics.

8. _____ was originally designed to produce business reports.

9. The programming language most widely used on microcomputers is _____.

10. Batch programs are placed in a(n) _____ to wait their turn to be executed.

SHORT ANSWER

1. What is an advantage of batch programming? What is an advantage of interactive programming?

2. Name one advantage and one disadvantage of assembly language.

3.   Compare the two machine-oriented languages discussed in
     this chapter.   Which one is easier to write programs in and
     why?

4.   Explain the difference between the modes an APL program may
     use.

5.   Give four reasons that COBOL is a popular business
     language.

6.   Why is Logo becoming a popular language to teach children?

7.   How are query languages most commonly used?

8.   What does it mean for a particular programming application
      to be input/output-bound?

9.   Name an advantage of FORTRAN.   Name two disadvantages.

10.   List and briefly explain the purpose of the four divisions
      of a COBOL program.

ANSWER KEY

True/False

1. F   3. T   5. F   7. T   9. F

Matching

1. i   3. h   5. f   7. j   9. d

Short Answer

1.   Batch programming can be used to make efficient use of
      computer time since programs can be executed during times
      when computer use isn't heavy. Interactive programming
      allows the user to obtain results immediately.

3.   Machine language consists of 0s and 1s and can be directly
      executed by the computer. Assembly language statements
      have a one-to-one correspondence to machine language and
      therefore are very easy to translate into machine language.
      They make use of mnemonics to represent machine operations.
      Also, labels can be used to represent storage locations.
      This makes assembly language programs easier to write than
      machine language programs.

5.   COBOL is a popular business language because

      ● it is English-like
      ● it is fairly easy to learn
      ● it has strong file-handling characteristics
      ● it is standardized

7.   Query languages are most commonly used to obtain an answer
      from a data base.

9.   FORTRAN is an excellent choice for doing mathematical
      computations. But it has only a limited ability to process
      alphabetic data and is not a good choice when dealing with
      large files.

Structured Design Concepts

KEY TERMS

Chief programmer team (CPT) – A method of organization used in the management of system projects where a chief programmer supervises the programming and testing of system modules; programmer productivity and system reliabilty are increased.

Detail diagram – Used in HIPO to describe the specific function performed or data items used in a module.

Dummy modules – A temporary program module that is inserted at a lower level prior to completion of coding of the higher-level modules to facilitate testing of higher-level modules.

Formal design review – Also called a structured walkthrough; an evaluation of the documentation of a system by a group of managers, analysts, and programmers to determine completeness, accuracy, and quality of design.

HIPO (Hierarchy plus Input-Process-Output) – A documentation technique used to describe the inputs, processing, and outputs of program modules.

Informal design review – An evaluation of system-designed documentation by selected management, analysts, and programmers prior to the actual coding of program modules to determine necessary additions, deletions, and modifications to the system design.

Librarian – Data-processing personnel responsible for the control and maintenance of files, programs, and catalogs; also responsible for subsequent processing or historical record-keeping.

Main control module – The highest level in the module hierarchy; controls other modules below it.

Modular approach – Simplifying a project by breaking it into segments or subunits.

Module – A part of a whole; a program segment; a subsystem.

Overview diagram – Used in HIPO to describe, in greater detail, a module shown in the visual table of contents.

Proper program – A program using the structured approach and top-down design, and having only one entrance and one exit.

Structure chart – A graphic representation of top-down programming; displaying modules of the problem solution and relationships between modules; of two types--system and process.

Structured programming – A top-down modular approach to programming that emphasizes dividing a program into logical sections in order to reduce testing time, increase programmer productivity, and bring clarity to programming.

Structured walkthrough – See Formal design review.

Top-down design – A method of defining a solution in terms of major functions to be performed, and further breaking down the major functions into subfunctions; the further the breakdown, the greater the detail.

Visual table of contents – Similar to a structure chart; each block is given an identification number that is used as a reference in other HIPO diagrams.

SUMMARY

Today software development lags far behind existing technology. Therefore, it is necessary for data processing departments to increase their productivity. The basic ways this can be done are: (1) to automate the software development process, (2) to require employees to work harder or longer or both, and (3) to change software development methodology. This chapter focuses on improving methodology. Three techniques can

be used to greatly improve software development methodology:
structured design, structured programming, and structured
review.

Top-down design is a form of structured design that refers
to the process of breaking a large problem down into its major
functions and then continuing to break each of these functions
down further. These individual functions are referred to as
modules.

The relationship between modules can be represented
graphically in a structure chart. Structure charts show
functions, their relationships, and the flow of control. They
must be supplemented with system charts, program flowcharts, and
record layouts to show processing flow and the order of
execution.

The term HIPO is used to describe a package which often is
used to supplement structure charts. The HIPO package usually
consists of three types of diagrams: a visual table of
contents, an overview diagram and a detail diagram. Pseudocode
is also often used to give a narrative description of a program
solution.

Structured programming is used to develop well-written
programs that have easy-to-follow logic patterns. The four
objectives of structured programming are:

- to reduce testing time
- to increase programming productivity
- to increase clarity by reducing complexity
- to decrease maintenance time and effort

Structured programs try to avoid using GOTO statements.
Languages that are well-suited to structured programming are
Pascal, PL/I, and COBOL.

A system design effort is often started by the formation of
a chief programmer team (CPT). This is a small group of
programmers led by a chief programmer who is responsible for the
overall coordination and success of the project. The CPT
includes a librarian to help maintain up-to-date documentation,
source-program listings, and test data. This helps members of
the team to keep track of how the project is developing.

Often an informal design review is done in the early phases
of system development. This allows selected personnel to
suggest modifications before coding of the program begins.
Later on, when the system is better documented, a formal design
review may take place. This is generally done by a team that

determines the overall completeness, accuracy, and quality of the design.

After a program is coded and executed, the output must be carefully checked for accuracy.

Egoless programming refers to the concept of reviewing programs to determine if they are coded consistently and follow predetermined standards. This encourages smooth program development and maintenance.

STRUCTURED LEARNING

1.   Top-down design always
      a.   works from the general to the specific
      b.   develops programs that work the first time
      c.   results in programs with no GOTO statements
      d.   can be used only with certain programs

      *   *   *   *   *   *   *   *   *   *

      (a) Using top-down design in developing problem solutions involves dealing with the major problems first. Once they are worked out, the problem is broken down into smaller units, leaving the minor details until the end. Programs written using this method generally have few GOTO statements, although some may still be necessary. Top-down design may be used when working with any programming language. Although top-down design helps to decrease errors in the final program, inevitably there will still be some errors.

2.   The flow of control in a structure chart
      a.   depends on the situation
      b.   goes from the bottom to the top
      c.   goes from the top to the bottom
      d.   goes from left to right

      *   *   *   *   *   *   *   *   *   *

      (c) The flow of control in a structure chart always goes from top to bottom. This clearly demonstrates the top-down design of the solution. The main control module is at the highest level and from there, every level represents modules of increasing detail.

3.   It is important that each module have only one entry point
      and one exit point because
      a.   this is the only way programs can be written
      b.   this makes the basic flow of logic easy to follow and
            allows for easy modifications
      c.   otherwise the program will not execute properly
      d.   it takes longer to write programs with several entries
            and exits

      *   *   *   *   *   *   *   *   *   *

      (b) Although programs may be written and will work
      properly with multiple entries and exits, program logic is
      improved and modification is made easier if there is only
      one of each.

4.   Generally, the optimum length for a module is
      a.   40-60 lines
      b.   less than 20 lines
      c.   100-200 lines
      d.   any length

      *   *   *   *   *   *   *   *   *   *

      (a) Keeping modules to a length of about 50-60 lines
      allows the module to be large enough to perform a
      particular function and yet small enough to fit on a single
      sheet of computer paper. This simplifies testing and
      debugging.

5.   Which of the following is not a rule that must be followed
      in top-down design?
      a.   Each module should be independent of the others.
      b.   Each module should be executed only when control is
            passed from the module directly above it.
      c.   After a module is executed, control should be passed
            back to the module directly above it.
      d.   No module may be executed more than once in a program.

      *   *   *   *   *   *   *   *   *   *

      (b) In top-down design, a module may be executed any
      number of times, depending on how often it is needed.
      However, control should be passed to it from the module
      directly above it and returned to that module after
      execution. These modules should be independent of one
      another.

6.   The purpose of a visual table of contents is to
     a.   give identification numbers to the parts of a structure
          chart so that these parts may be referred to later
     b.   list the pseudocode of a program
     c.   give a flowchart of a program
     d.   describe each data item used by a program

     *   *   *   *   *   *   *   *   *   *

     (a) A visual table of contents assigns identification num-
     bers to parts of a structure chart so that these parts may
     be referenced later. It is not a flowchart or pseudocode
     since it simply shows the hierarchical ordering of the
     program modules. It does not deal with identifying data
     items needed by particular modules.

7.   An overview diagram is used to
     a.   describe a module
     b.   explain the overall purpose of a program
     c.   give a narrative description of the logic of a program
     d.   visually represent the logic of an entire program

     *   *   *   *   *   *   *   *   *   *

     (a) Overview diagrams describe modules by listing the
     module's inputs, processing, and outputs. They do not deal
     with the program as an entire unit. There is one overview
     diagram for each module in a program.

8.   Because the cost of programmers' time is increasing while
     the cost of hardware is decreasing, it is important that
     a.   programmers work long hours
     b.   all programs are thoroughly tested
     c.   the programmers' time is used efficiently
     d.   all programmers work on teams

     *   *   *   *   *   *   *   *   *   *

     (c) Because the cost of programmers' time is always
     increasing, it is important that their time be used in the
     most effective way.

9.   Egoless programming can improve the quality of programs
      being written by
      a.   having a librarian for each chief programmer team
      b.   requiring all programmers to use structure charts when
            developing a problem solution
      c.   requiring programs to go through an informal design
            review
      d.   making sure all programs maintain certain predefined
            coding standards.

      *   *   *   *   *   *   *   *   *   *

      (d) Egoless programming refers to the practice of reviewing
      all programs written to determine if they meet certain
      predefined standards. While the first three choices
      may increase the quality of the finished program and
      help to make the programmer's time well-spent, they are
      not directly involved in the idea of egoless
      programming.

10.   Which of the following is not one of the three major struc-
      tured techniques used to develop programs efficiently?
      a.   structured programming
      b.   structured design
      c.   structured review
      d.   structured walkthrough

      *   *   *   *   *   *   *   *   *   *

      (d) A structured walkthrough is a method of evaluating a
      system design effort to determine if it is complete and
      well-done. It may be used as a part of a structured
      review. Structured design, programming, and review are the
      three major structured techniques used in program develop-
      ment discussed in this chapter.

TRUE/FALSE

1.   T F   The modular approach to problem solving refers to
              breaking the problem into segments.

2.   T F   Structured programs generally contain many branches.

3.   T F   When writing structured programs, it is important to
              keep modules fairly small.

4.   T F   Software development is not labor intensive.

5.   T   F   An informal design review is held after a program is
              completely coded.

6.   T   F   An overview diagram includes a module's inputs,
              processing, and output.

7.   T   F   In a structure chart, the main control module is at
              the highest level.

8.   T   F   Egoless programming is a concept involving the
              review of programs to determine if they meet certain
              predefined standards.

9.   T   F   Structured programming leads to programs with logic
              that is difficult to follow.

10. T   F   Companies should establish programming standards and
              require that certain programs written by their
              employees follow these standards.

MATCHING

a.   structure chart   f.   structured programming
b.   chief programmer   g.   librarian
c.   hardware   h.   CPT
d.   module   i.   overview
e.   structured walkthrough   j.   proper program

1.   A single step in the solution to a problem is a(n) _____.

2.   A(n) _____ graphically depicts how the modules of a
     problem solution are related.

3.   A program with only one entrance and one exit is a(n)
     _____.

4.   A(n) _____ helps to maintain complete, up-to-date docu-
     mentation on a programming project.

5.   The supervisor of a CPT is referred to as the _____.

6.   A formal design review may also be called a(n) _____.

7.   Software now accounts for a larger share of data-processing
     budgets than _____.

8.   _____ diagrams show the input, processing steps, and out-
      put of a given module.

9.   _____ is sometimes referred to as "GOTO-less"
      programming.

10.   A group of programmers working on a software development
      project is called a(n) _____.

SHORT ANSWER

1.   List three ways data processing departments can increase
      their efficiency.

2.   Name three structured techniques that can be useful in
      developing programs.

3.   How can top-down designs improve programmer efficiency?

4.   What does HIPO stand for? What might be included in a HIPO
     package?

5.   Why is structured programming sometimes referred to as
     "GOTO-less programming?

6.   List the titles of three people who will often be on a
     chief programmer team.

7.   Explain what is meant by the term egoless programming.

8.   How are dummy modules useful in testing structured programs?

9.   Name three programming languages that are well-suited to structured programming.

10.   At what point in a system design development project might an informal review take place? When might there be a formal design review?

ANSWER KEY

True/False

1. T   3. T   5. F   7. T   9. F

Matching

1. d   3. j   5. b   7. c   9. f

Short Answer

1. Three ways data processing departments can increase their efficiency are to:

   • automate the software development process
   • require employees to work harder or longer or both
   • change software development methodologies

3. Top-down design can increase programmer efficiency because it makes the programmer deal with the major problems first and then figure out how to handle minor problems and specify the actual coding. This leads to programs with efficiently developed logic patterns.

5. Structured programming attempts to keep branches, often referred to as GOTO statements, to a minimum. Numerous branches can make program logic difficult to follow and may make the modification of a program needlessly complex.

7. Egoless programming attempts to maintain a predefined standard of programming in all programs written. This encourages programmers to work as a unit and to think of problems that may occur when others need to use or modify their programs. It encourages uniformity among all programs.

9. COBOL, PL/I, and Pascal

Application Software

KEY TERMS

Cell – The unique location within an electronic spreadsheet where a row and a column intersect.

Command area – The area at the bottom of some electronic spreadsheets that displays the available commands to the user.

Cursor – Usually a flashing character such as an underline or a block that shows where the next typed character will appear on the computer display screen.

Data base – The cornerstone of a management information system; basic data are commonly defined and consistently organized to fit the information needs of a wide variety of users in an organization.

Dedicated word-processing system – A computer system designed solely for the purpose of word processing.

Deletion – A word processing feature that allows removal of characters, words, sentences, or blocks of text.

Document-oriented word processor – A word processor that treats a text file as a document, rather than as a series of pages; a greater portion of the file is held in primary storage thereby reducing the amount of secondary storage accessing that must be done.

Electronic spreadsheet – An electronic ledger sheet used to store and manipulate any type of numerical data.

File handlers – A data manager application package which is capable of operating on only one file at a time.

Graphics software packages – Application software packages designed to allow the user to display images on the display screen or a printer.

Horizontal software integration – In a business sense, application software packages that are general in nature and can be used for a variety of applications; in a design sense, the combination of various types of application software packages.

Insertion – A word processing feature that allows characters, words, sentences, or blocks of text to be inserted into a document.

Line editor – A word processor that allows the user to operate on only one line of text at a time; contrast to a screen editor.

Model – A representation of a real-world system; used to construct a decision support system to help managers with their decision-making tasks.

Modeling package – An application software program incorporating a representation of a real-world system developed by a manager and manager's staff.

Page-oriented word processor – A word processor that treats a document as a series of pages; contrast to document-oriented word processor.

Pixels – The individual dots on a display screen that are used to create characters and images.

Print formatting – The process in which the word processor communicates with the printer indicating how the text should be printed.

Screen editor – A word processor that allows for the editing of text that appears on the entire display screen; contrast with a line editor.

Screen formatting – Features within a word processor that control the way in which text appears on the display screen.

Scrolling – The process of positioning a portion of a text file onto the display screen; used to view portions of a document while using a word processor.

Search – A word-processing feature that allows the user to specify a word or set of characters that need to be located throughout the document.

Simulation – The process used by decision-support-system users to gain insight into the workings of an actual system.

Spreadsheet – Also known as a ledger sheet; used by accountants for performing financial calculations and recording transactions.

Status area – A portion of an electronic spreadsheet that appears at the top of the display and shows the location of the cursor within the spreadsheet and what was entered into a particular cell of the spreadsheet.

Template – A predefined set of formulas for use on an electronic spreadsheet.

Text-editing – Using a word processor to enter and store a text file in the computer's secondary storage and then retrieve it for editing and storing as the old file, or as a new file.

Undo – A word-processing feature that allows the user to recover text that has been accidentally deleted.

Vertical software integration – In a business sense, a software package designed for a specific purpose such as legal word processing; in a design sense, the enhancement of a single package.

Window – See Window environment.

Window environment – An operating system enhancement that allows more than one application software package to run concurrently.

Word processing – Using a computer to perform text-editing and formatting.

Word processor – An application software package that performs text-editing functions.

Word wrap – Also known as word wraparound; a word-processing feature that automatically positions text so full words are positioned within declared margins.

Word-processing system – A computer system on which word processing can be performed; of two types--a dedicated word processor and a word processor used on a general-purpose computer system.

SUMMARY

The number of prewritten software packages has increased because of the rising cost of developing application software and the rise in popularity of microcomputers. The four most popular types of packages are word processing, data-management, modeling, and graphics packages.

A word processor is a package designed to allow the user to enter, manipulate, format, print, store, and retrieve text. Word-processing systems can be either one of two configurations. A dedicated word processing system is used only for word processing. A multipurpose digital computer can have a word processor plus other application software packages.

Word processing involves two steps. The first, text-editing, enables the user to enter text into the computer, store it, edit it, and save the new version. Text can be edited in two ways. A line editor allows editing of only one line at a time while a screen editor can be used to edit an entire screen of text at once. The second step of word processing is print formatting, telling the computer how to print the text.

Common features offered on most word processors are: 1) writing and editing, 2) screen formatting, and 3) print formatting. Writing and editing include positioning the cursor, word wrap, scrolling, insertion and deletion, move, search, and undo. Screen formatting features control the way text is displayed on the screen. Print formatting features include margin settings, line spacing, centering, automatic pagination, headers and footers, and character enhancements.

The two types of data managers (data-management packages), file handlers and data base packages, both computerize the tasks of recording and filing information. File handlers were developed to replace manual filing systems. Only one data file can be accessed at a time. Data base packages consolidate independent files into one data base so that all users can access the files.

Standard features offered by most data managers include: adding and deleting records, searching for and/or updating records, sorting data files, printing files and making mathematical calculations.

A model is a mathematical representation of a real world situation. Modeling software uses the power and speed of a computer to peform mathematical calculations. Modeling software is popularly used to help business managers make decisions.

An electronic spreadsheet is a computerized version of a traditional spreadsheet, a table of rows and columns used to store and manipulate any kind of numerical data. A cell is the location on a spreadsheet where a certain row and column meet. Cells can contain labels, values, or formulas.

Graphics software packages are designed to allow the user to display images on a computer monitor or to print images on a printer. Pixels, individual dots on the screen, are combined to create characters or images. Graphics packages are used in business to summarize data in charts or graphs and to help design products and parts.

Software integration can be viewed in two ways. From a business-oriented perspective, software integration refers to the purpose for which the software was designed. Horizontal software integration refers to general packages that can be used for various types of applications. Vertical software integration indicates packages that are designed for a special purpose.

From the software design perspective, horizontal integration describes a combination of application packages that can be used together. Vertical integration refers to the enhancement of a single package.

Windows, or window environments, allow more than one application package to run concurrently. An individual package such as word processor or data manager is available to the user at all times.

STRUCTURED LEARNING

1.   The purpose of the text-editing function of a word processor is to
      a.   enter data into the computer
      b.   determine subscripts and superscripts
      c.   underline and boldface certain words
      d.   both a and c

      *   *   *   *   *   *   *   *   *   *

(a) Entering data is the only text-editing function listed. Both b and c are functions of print formatting.

2. Common features offered in almost all word processing packages include all but which one of the following?
    a.   animation
    b.   writing and editing
    c.   screen formatting
    d.   print formatting

    *   *   *   *   *   *   *   *   *   *

    (a) Animation is a feature of graphics software packages.

3. Which of the following can be used to computerize recording and filing information?
    a.   electronic spreadsheets   c.   file handlers
    b.   data base packages   d.   both b and c

    *   *   *   *   *   *   *   *   *   *

    (d) Data base packages and file handlers are both data managers used to replace traditional filing systems.

4. Which data manager feature would you use if you wanted to make a list of all students in a student enrollment file who had not paid this term's tuition?
    a.   add/delete   c.   sort
    b.   list   d.   search/update

    *   *   *   *   *   *   *   *   *   *

    (d) The search/update feature can search an existing file for the records of students marked as unpaid. Sort and add/delete are also data manager functions while list is not.

5. What type of application software would be most helpful in manipulating large amounts of financial information in various ways?
    a.   dedicated word processor
    b.   electronic spreadsheet
    c.   file handler
    d.   financial data manager

    *   *   *   *   *   *   *   *   *   *

(b) Electronic spreadsheets can facilitate the tasks of preparing financial reports and recording transactions by quickly calculating changes.

6. Which of the following features is not a feature common to software packages?
    a. two- and three-dimensional display
    b. automatic spillover
    c. high resolution
    d. cursor positioning

    *   *   *   *   *   *   *   *   *   *

    (b) Automatic spillover is a feature of some electronic spreadsheets which allows extra-long labels to spill over into the next cell.

7. A data manager software package designed to maintain the inventory records of a women's clothing store would be
    a. dedicated
    b. horizontally integrated
    c. vertically integrated
    d. simulated

    *   *   *   *   *   *   *   *   *   *

    (c) Vertical software integration refers to software designed for a specific purpose like inventory control for a specialized clothing store.

8. The type of word processing sytems used on multipurpose digital computers
    a. are used only for word processing by businesses requiring large quantities of word processing to be done
    b. are used by businesses desiring to use more than one single application
    c. is called a dedicated word processing system
    d. none of the above

    *   *   *   *   *   *   *   *   *   *

    (b) Dedicated word processing systems are designed only for word processing and are usually found in businesses where large quantities of word processing must be done.

9.   The edit mode of a word processor
     a.   allows the user to enter text
     b.   allows the user to change text
     c.   permits one page of text to be in internal memory at a
          time
     d.   both a and b

*   *   *   *   *   *   *   *   *   *

(b) The edit mode permits editing of a document.

10. Scrolling
     a.   allows the user to position a particular portion of
          text file onto the display screen
     b.   allows the user to move through a document from top to
          bottom
     c.   allows the user to move the document on the display
          screen horizontally
     d.   all of the above

*   *   *   *   *   *   *   *   *   *

(d) Scrolling positions a portion of text onto the display
screen and can be done either horizontally or vertically.

TRUE/FALSE

1.   T   F   A screen editor treats a text file as one single
             document, eliminating the need to work on pages
             separately.

2.   T   F   Features of print formatting in a word processing
             package are being able to indicate automatic page
             numbering and underlining and boldfacing.

3.   T   F   The window is a blinking line or box on the display
             screen used to show the current position on the
             display.

4.   T   F   All data managers can sort information in some order
             and update information within a file.

5.   T   F   Data bases consolidate various independent files
             into one integrated whole, so all users can have
             access to the information they need.

6.   T F   File handlers, for the most part, offer limited
              mathematical capabilities while data base management
              packages permit more complex computations.

7.   T F   Simulation is one type of graphics software package.

8.   T F   In an electronic spreadsheet, it is possible to pre-
              vent the contents of certain cells from being
              displayed.

9.   T F   High-resolution graphics have a greater total number
              of pixels on the display screen, thus creating
              sharper images.

10.   T F   Advantages of windows over conventional application
              packages are: the ability to transfer data between
              software applications and the capability to provide
              consistent command structure.

MATCHING

a. window   f. vertical software
b. help screen   integration
c. model   g. template
d. scrolling   h. cell
e. dedicated   i. pixels
                              j. horizontal software
                                  integration

1.   _____ allows the user to position a certain segment of
      the text onto the display screen.

2.   When a user would like to know which choices are available
      at a certain point in the program, a(n) _____ can display
      the options and sometimes, an explanation of each.

3.   A predefined set of formulas used with electronic
      spreadsheets is called a(n) _____.

4.   In the business sense, _____ refers to software packages
      that can be used for a number of different purposes.

5.   A(n) _____ is a mathematical representation of a real
      world situation.

6.   A word-processing system that is used only for word proc-
      essing is said to be _____.

7.   A unique location within a spreadsheet, or _____, is the point where a row and a column meet.

8.   A software package that allows more than one application package to run concurrently is a(n) _____.

9.   In the business sense, _____ refers to software packages designed for a specific purpose.

10. In graphics packages, the individual dots on the display screen that create characters and images are called _____.

SHORT ANSWER

1.   Explain the two steps involved in word processing.

2.   How do file handlers and data base packages differ in their capabilities?

3.   List some uses of data managers in the home.

4.   What two factors are responsible for increasing the use of prewritten application software packages?

5.   What advantages does a document-oriented word processor have over a page-oriented word processor?

6.   List five common writing and editing features of word processors.

7.   How can the search features of a word processor help a user when writing and editing text?

8.   Explain how modeling software can be used in the business
      environment.

9.   What are the main uses of graphics software packages?

10.   Differentiate between horizontal and vertical software
      integration, from the business-oriented perspective.

ANSWER KEY

True/False

1.   F   3. F   5. T   7. F   9. T

Matching

1.   d   3. g   5. c   7. h   9. f

Short Answer

1. Text-editing and print formatting are the two steps in word processing. Text-editing allows the user to enter data into the computer, store it, and later edit it, saving the new version. Print formatting tells the computer how to print the text.

3. Data managers can be used in the home to create com-puterized Christmas card lists, address books, phone listings, recipe card files, or mailing lists. They can also help balance checkbooks, keep personal property inven-tories, keep appointment calendars, or keep track of books in a personal library.

5. A document-oriented word processor eliminates the need to work on pages separately. It also allows a larger portion of a file to be held in internal memory, reducing the number of times secondary storage must be accessed.

7. The user can indicate a word or set of characters for the word processor to find. The cursor will automatically be positioned at the first character of the string when it is located. The user may also instruct the word processor to replace the string with another one every time it is found in the text.

9. Graphics packages can be used in business to produce graphs and charts, and to aid in designing objects and parts. In art, this software can be used to paint images or pictures on the display screen. Graphics packages are also used in the design process of computer video games to create display screens.

System Analysis and Design

KEY TERMS

Action entry – One of four sections of a decision logic table; specifies what actions should be taken.

Action stub – One of four sections of a decision logic table; describes possible actions applicable to the problem to be solved.

Condition entry – One of four sections of a decision logic table; answers all questions in the condition stub.

Condition stub – one of four sections of a decision logic table; describes all factors (options) to be considered in determining a course of action.

Crash (direct) conversion – Also known as direct conversion; a method of system implementation in which the old system is abandoned and the new one implemented at once.

Decision logic table (DLT) – A standardized table that organizes relevant facts in a clear and concise manner to aid in the decision-making process.

Edit checks – Program statements designed to test data that are entered as input to a program for such things as reasonableness; a very critical part of online applications where information is updated immediately.

Feedback – A check within a system to see whether or not predetermined goals are being met.

161

Grid chart – A chart used in system analysis and design to summarize the relationship between the components of a system.

Input – Data that are submitted to the computer for processing.

Menu-driven – An application program is said to be menu-driven when it provides the user with "menus" displaying available choices or selections to help guide the user through the process of using the software package.

Online storage symbol (▱) – A symbol that indicates the file is kept on an online external storage medium such as disk or tape.

Output – Information that comes from the computer as a result of processing.

Parallel conversion – A system implementation approach in which the new system is operated side-by-side with the old one until all differences are reconciled.

Phased conversion – A method of system implementation in which the old system is gradually replaced by the new one; the new system is segmented and gradually applied.

Pilot conversion – The implementation of a new system into the organization on a piecemeal basis; also known as modular conversion.

Process – To transform raw data into useful information.

System – A group of related elements that work together toward a common goal.

System analysis – A detailed, step-by-step investigation of an organization and its systems for the purpose of determining what must be done in relation to the system and the best way to do it.

System analysis report – A report given to top management after the system analysis phase has been completed to report the findings of the system study; includes a statement of objectives, constraints, and possible alternatives.

System design report – A report given to top management after the system analysis phase that explains how various designs will satisfy the information requirements; includes flowcharts, narratives, resources required to implement alternatives, and recommendations.

System flowchart – The group of symbols to represent the general information flow; focuses on inputs and outputs rather than on internal computer operations.

Tabular chart – See Grid chart.

User friendly – An easy-to-use, understandable software design that makes it easy for noncomputer personnel to use an application software package.

SUMMARY

System analysis and design is an approach used to develop and maintain information systems that supply managers in an organization with needed information.

A system is a group of related elements that work together toward a common goal. The four components of a system are inputs, processes, outputs, and feedback. Most systems are collections of subsystems and are themselves subsystems of larger systems. An important concept of system theory is that systems are not isolated; there is interaction among them.

In order for a system analyst to determine the information needs of an organization, certain tools must be used to analyze the entire organization. The systems approach tries to mirror the actual events while reducing the complexity. The systems model only highlights the important relationships, patterns, and flows of information.

The system approach views an organization as an integrated whole, not as groups of independent functional areas. This entails viewing the organization from the top down.

The development of a new information system involves the following steps: analysis, design, programming, implementation, and audit and review.

System analysis consists of formulating a statement of overall business objectives, gaining a general understanding of the scope of the problem, and making a proposal to conduct system analysis to management. Once the proposal is accepted, the next step is to gather data, and finally, to draw up the findings as a report.

Data gathering includes collecting data about the current
system. Internal sources include personal interviews, system
flowcharts, questionnaires, and formal reports. Sources outside
the organization can include books, periodicals, product speci-
fications, customers, suppliers, and competitors.

The analyst should analyze data so as to gain an understanding of the system. Grid charts, system flowcharts, and
decision logic tables are tools that can be used to facilitate
the analysis.

The second phase of system development is the design of
alternative systems that will meet the information needs. The
steps of system design are: review goals and objectives,
develop a model of the system, evaluate constraints, develop
alternative designs, perform a feasibility analysis and a
cost/benefit analysis, and prepare a system design report and
recommendation.

The third phase is system programming which can be very
time consuming. After each program module is completed, it
should be tested. When all program testing is done, the entire
system should be tested. This phase should not neglect system
documentation which reviews the purpose of the entire system,
its subsystems, and the function of each subsystem. Documentation includes system flowcharts depicting the major processsing
flows, and the input and output forms.

After a design has been approved, the fourth stage, implementation, can begin. Implementation includes training the computer operators and also the users of the system. During this
stage, the switch from the old processing mode, equipment, and
clerical procedures to the new system must be made. This switch
can be accomplished in several ways: parallel conversion, pilot
conversion, phased conversion, or crash conversion.

The final stage is system audit and review. The analyst
gets feedback on the system's performance to see if the objectives are being met. If they are not, some changes and improvements may be needed.

STRUCTURED LEARNING

1. Which of the following would not be a valid reason for
    reviewing a current information system?
    a. Government has imposed a new regulation.
    b. A development in technology has occurred.
    c. There is a need to solve a problem.
    d. The MIS department's workload has decreased.

    *   *   *   *   *   *   *   *   *   *

    (d) Reviewing a current information system can be costly
    and time-consuming. Trying to make work for the MIS
    department is not a reason to undertake such an endeavor.

2. The first step in a system analysis is
    a. to formulate a statement of system objectives
    b. to prepare design alternatives for management review
    c. to purchase the necessary hardware
    d. to collect data

    *   *   *   *   *   *   *   *   *   *

    (a) The formulation of a statement of system objectives is
    essential to the identification of information require-
    ments. Based on these objectives, the analyst can gain a
    general understanding of what must be done.

3. The tools used in data analysis include
    a. grid charts   d. system flowcharts
    b. decision logic tables   e. all of the above
    c. program flowcharts   f. a, b, and d

    *   *   *   *   *   *   *   *   *   *

    (f) Grid charts, decision logic tables, and system
    flowcharts are important tools used in data analysis.
    Program flowcharts do not specifically identify input and
    output forms, things a system analyst needs to know.

4.   The condition entry of a decision logic table
      a.   signals the channel to enter another program into
           internal memory
      b.   describes all conditions that need to be considered
      c.   describes the possible actions to be taken if the con-
           dition is true
      d.   summarizes the relationship among the parts of a
           system

      *   *   *   *   *   *   *   *   *   *

      (b) The condition entry is a basic component of a decision
      logic table. It contains all the conditions that have been
      determined to be necessary to permit a decision to be made
      in a specific situation.

5.   When analyzing design alternatives, the analyst
      a.   should concentrate on quantitative methods
      b.   should carefully evaluate qualitative factors
      c.   all of the above
      d.   none of the above

      *   *   *   *   *   *   *   *   *   *

      (c) Design alternatives encompass both qualitative and
      quantitative factors. The analyst must include all impor-
      tant decisions in the design alternative if the system is
      to be successful.

6.   The final step in system design is
      a.   a cost/benefit analysis
      b.   a system recommendation
      c.   system selection
      d.   evaluating organization constraints

      *   *   *   *   *   *   *   *   *   *

      (b) The system recommendation is the final step of system
      design. At this point, the analyst presents to management
      the design that he/she feels would most effectively
      accomplish the objectives of the system.

7.   A conversion technique that involves initially converting
      only a small part of the organization to the new system is
      a.   parallel conversion   c.   phased conversion
      b.   pilot conversion   d.   direct conversion

      *   *   *   *   *   *   *   *   *   *

(b) Pilot conversion converts one part of the organization to the new system at a time. This helps to identify problems before the system is completely converted.

8. The most risky conversion method is
    a. parallel conversion   c. phased conversion
    b. pilot conversion   d. direct conversion

    *   *   *   *   *   *   *   *   *   *

    (d) Direct, or crash, conversion takes place all at once. The old system is discontinued immediately upon implemen- tation of the new one. If problems arise, the organization has nothing to fall back on.

9. The following edit checks should be incorporated into the solution design.
    a. reasonableness checks   d. both a and b
    b. monetary checks   e. both a and c
    c. range checks

    *   *   *   *   *   *   *   *   *   *

    (e) Edit checks can be of several types: reasonableness, range, type, and correct code. Monetary checks are not edit checks.

10. One of the most important tasks during system audit and review is
    a. to educate the users of the system
    b. to ensure that all system controls are working properly
    c. to completely document the system
    d. all of the above

    *   *   *   *   *   *   *   *   *   *

    (b) System audit and review should ensure that all system controls are working properly. Educating the users is part of implementation and documenting the system is part of system programming.

TRUE/FALSE

1. T F The system approach involves viewing an organization by its individual functional areas.

2.   T   F   The focus during data collection is on what is being
              done, whereas the focus during data analysis is on
              why certain operations and procedures are being
              used.

3.   T   F   System flowcharts are designed to represent the
              detailed flow of information, using many different
              process symbols to show each operation.

4.   T   F   System analysis should try to develop more than one
              alternative when designing a complex information
              system.

5.   T   F   When conducting a cost/benefit analysis, it is
              generally easier to determine costs than benefits.

6.   T   F   It is only necessary to perform a cost/benefit
              analysis on the system design the analyst recommends
              to management.

7.   T   F   Computerized information systems are always more
              efficient than manual information systems.

8.   T   F   The inputs for a new information system can be
              determined by examining the required outputs.

9.   T   F   The goal of system implementation is to ensure that
              the system is completely debugged, operational, and
              accepted by the users.

10.   T   F   After a system has been installed, nothing more has
              to be done.

MATCHING

        a.   flexible   f.   documentation
        b.   parallel   g.   decision makers
        c.   action stub   h.   proposal
        d.   grid chart   i.   condition stub
        e.   users   j.   pilot

1.   A(n) _____ is a decision logic table that describes the
      different criteria the decision-maker may encounter.

2.   The purpose of a(n) _____ is to determine if a need
      exists for conducting a system analysis.

3.   _____ of a system has historically been neglected.

4.   The conversion process in which the new system is run along with the old system for some time is _____ .

5.   During training, both operators and _____ must be educated about the system.

6.   A tabular representation used to summarize relationships is called a(n) _____ .

7.   The conversion method which involves converting only part of the organization to the new system is _____ .

8.   An information system is designed to satisfy the needs of _____ .

9.   In a decision logic table, the _____ describes possible events that the decision-maker could cause to occur.

10.   A well-designed system should be _____ and adaptable.

SHORT ANSWER

1.   Explain the four components of a system.

2.   What are the steps in developing an information system?

3.   What should be included in a proposal to conduct system
      analysis?

4.   When is a decision logic table a valuable tool for ana-
      lyzing data?

5.   When does the system design stage begin? What should the
      analyst concentrate on during this stage?

6.   List the organizational constraints an analyst must con-
      sider when designing information system alternatives.

7.   Why do the information needs of an organization change?

8.   List and explain the four types of edit checks designed to
      identify potential errors in the input data.

9.   What are some of the factors that should be considered when
      developing alternative information system designs?

10.   What is a feasibility study?

ANSWER KEY

True/False

1. F   3. F   5. T   7. F   9. T

Matching

1. i   3. f   5. e   7. j   9. c

Short Answer

1.   Inputs enter the system and are transformed by some process
     into outputs. Feedback informs the system if predetermined
     standards or goals are being met.

3.   A clear and concise statement of the problem or reason for
     system analysis. A statement defining the objectives of
     the system analysis. An identification of the data that
     must be collected and the sources of this data. A schedule
     for conducting the analysis.

5.   The system design stage begins after management has
     reviewed the system analysis report and agrees to continue
     the project. The analyst should focus on how a system can
     be developed to meet the information requirements.

7.   Information needs change because an organization changes.
     Some factors creating change are growth, new requirements,
     new technology, government regulations, and environmental
     change.

9.   Important factors for consideration during system design
     include: the structures and formats of output reports, the
     program specifications needed to guide the programmer in
     code preparation, the data bases or files required, the
     clerical procedures that will be used, and the process-
     control measures that should be instituted.

File Organization and Data Design

KEY TERMS

Activity – Refers to the proportion of records accessed during an update run of the data file.

Attributes – A field containing information; a descriptive property associated with a name to describe a characteristic of items that the name may represent.

Batch processing – The grouping of user jobs for processing one after another in a continuous stream--a batch processing environment.

Data base – The cornerstone of a management information system; basic data are commonly defined and consistently organized to fit the information needs of a wide variety of users in an organization.

Data set – A grouping of related records; also called a file.

Data-base management system (DBMS) – A set of programs that serves as an interface between the data base and three principal users--the programmer, the operating system, and the user; provides a method of arranging data to limit duplication, an ability to make changes easily, and a capability to handle direct inquiries.

Directory – Consists of two columns, the first containing the key of the record and the second containing the address of the record with that key.

Field – A meaningful item of data, such as a social security number.

File – A grouping of related records; sometimes referred to as a data set.

Hashing – See Randomize.

Hierarchical structure – A method of organizing data within a data base that consists of one owner record and any number of member records.

Index – An ordered reference list of the contents of a file, or the keys for identification or location of the contents.

Indexed-sequential design – A file organization design that allows for both sequential access and direct access of data records.

Inverted structure – A file structure that permits fast, spontaneous searching for previously unspecified information; independent lists are maintained in record keys which are accessible to the value of specified fields.

Key – A unique identifier for a record; used to sort records for processing or to locate a particular record within a file.

Linear structure – A specific, ordered sequence of data records within a data base.

List – See Simple structure.

Logical design – The way in which data elements are arranged within a data base; independent of physical design.

Master file – A file that contains relatively permanent data; updated by records in a transaction file.

Physical design – Refers to how the data within a data base are kept on storage devices and how they are accessed.

Randomize – To compute record numbers from actual keys through any of a number of mathematical techniques.

Record – A collection of data items, or fields, that relates to a single unit.

Sequential file – Data (records) stored in specific order, one right after the other.

Sequential processing – See Batch processing.

Simple structure – A sequential arrangement of data records within a data base.

Transaction file – A file that contains new records or modifications to existing records; used to update a master file.

Tree structure – See Hierarchical structure.

Updating – Transferring new information from a transaction file to a master file by computer matching the two files.

Volatility – Refers to the number of changes that are made to a file over a certain time period.

SUMMARY

Files are widely used by all kinds of businesses. The type of file used by a particular organization depends on its needs. Three types of file design are covered in this chapter: sequential, direct-access, and indexed-sequential.

A file consists of a grouping of related records. File processing generally refers to the operation of updating permanent files to reflect changes in data. Historically, this has been done manually, but a great deal of time can be saved in doing it by computer.

Sequential files are arranged in order by a key, which is a field that can be used to uniquely identify a particular record. When updating a sequential file, the existing file, called the master file, and the file containing any changes to be made, called the transaction file, are used. The computer reads the two files sequentially, checking to see if the key fields match. If they do, the record information on the transaction file is copied to the new file in place of the old master record. If there is no transaction record for a given master record, the old master record is simply copied to the new file. In this way, a new master file is generated.

This method is excellent in situations where most of the records in a file need to be read and/or updated. The files can be stored inexpensively on magnetic tape and file design is simple. But, when doing sequential processing the entire file must be processed and the transactions must be sorted in a par-

ticular order. Also, a major disadvantage is that a particular
record cannot be accessed directly.

Direct-access design, on the other hand, allows for a particular record to be accessed and/or updated without the preceding records in the file being read. This is a good method
of dealing with files with low activity and high volatility.
These files must be on magnetic disk and need not be arranged in
any particular order.

Two methods may be used to access a particular record:
randomizing (also called hashing) and searching a directory.
Randomizing involves locating a record's address by performing
an arithmetic manipulation on the key field of the record. This
results in a disk address. One problem with this method is that
the address may not always be unique. When duplicate addresses
are generated, a routine must be available to deal with this
problem. Directories list the key field of records along with
their correct disk addresses. Direct-access design is excellent
for quickly locating a particular record, but does not lend
itself to sequential processing and can be complex to implement.

Files with indexed-sequential design allow the user to
directly access a particular record and also to sequentially
access the entire file. Consequently, this method is useful in
a wide variety of applications. An index (or directory) is used
to allow for direct access. Generally, direct access does not
directly locate the record needed, but locates the general area
of that record. Records must then be sequentially searched
until the correct record is located.

Data bases combine the files of an organization into a
central collection which can then be accessed by a wide variety
of users. This decreases duplication of data. Also, when
records need updating, there is no need to update several different files. The physical design of a data base refers to the
way in which data is arranged on storage devices. The logical
design refers to how this same data is viewed by application
programs and individual users.

Data in the data base can be easily arranged to suit the
needs of a particular user. Data base systems use direct-access
storage devices to retrieve records. Records may be arranged in
simple structures, linear structures, or hierarchical structures. Inverted structures may also be used to index selected
attributes in a file.

Data base management systems consist of a set of programs
to serve as an interface between the data base and the user.
These systems allow for a great deal of independence between the
data base and the application programs. Although data bases are

very useful, their implementation and maintenance require a
great deal of skill.

STRUCTURED LEARNING

1.   When updating a sequential file, the input files needed are
     the old master file and the
     a.   new master file   c.   transaction file
     b.   data base   d.   directory

     *   *   *   *   *   *   *   *   *   *

     (c) The old master file and the transaction file are used
     to make the new master file. The data base is a central
     collection of data, while a directory is used to access an
     indexed-sequential file.

2.   Sequential processing is generally considered to be effi-
     cient when
     a.   it is necessary to directly access records in a file
          frequently
     b.   the files must be stored on magnetic disks
     c.   at least half of the records are updated during a given
          processing run
     d.   both random access and direct access of a file are
          frequently needed

     *   *   *   *   *   *   *   *   *   *

     (c) When half or more of the records in a file need to be
     updated on any given run, sequentially accessing the file
     is problably the most efficient method. These files are
     stored on tape and may not be accessed directly.

3.   Before a file may be sequentially processed
     a.   the file must be in order by a particular field, called
          the key
     b.   neither field need be in any particular order
     c.   only the transaction file need be in order by the key
     d.   only the master file need be in order by the key

     *   *   *   *   *   *   *   *   *   *

     (a) For a file to be updated, both the master file and the
     transaction file need to be in order by the key field.

4.   A problem with using randomizing when accessing a record is
      that
      a.   it is a time-consuming way of locating a record
      b.   it may not always result in a unique address
      c.   it can be used only with files that are stored on tape
      d.   it cannot be used with direct-access files

      *   *   *   *   *   *   *   *   *   *

      (b) Randomizing is a fast, efficient way of directly
      accessing files stored on disk, but may not always give a
      unique disk address.

5.   If a file has high activity but low volatility, which
      method of file design would be most appropriate?
      a.   sequential   c.   indexed-sequential
      b.   direct-access   d.   linear

      *   *   *   *   *   *   *   *   *   *

      (a) Activity refers to the portion of records processed
      during an updating run and volatility refers to how fre-
      quently changes to a file are made. Therefore, a file with
      high activity and low volatility is suitable for sequential
      processing.

6.   Which of the following would not be considered a user of a
      data base?
      a.   programmer
      b.   operating system
      c.   user (the person searching the data base)
      d.   the data-base management system

      *   *   *   *   *   *   *   *   *   *

      (d) The data-base management system serves as an interface
      between the various users and the data base. Common users
      of data bases are programmers, operating systems and the
      users, those people who access the data base to obtain
      information.

7.   A disadvantage of the direct-access design is
      a.   it is slow
      b.   it does not allow a particular record to be located
           without reading every record before it
      c.   it is fairly complex
      d.   it is usually inflexible when dealing with inquiries

      *   *   *   *   *   *   *   *   *   *

(c) Although direct-access files are fairly flexible and quickly access the needed record, they are complex and can be difficult to implement.

8. Indexed-sequential files are useful because
    a. they cut down on duplication of data
    b. they are the fastest method of directly accessing a record
    c. they are the cheapest method of file design discussed
    d. they allow for both direct access and sequential processing of files

    *   *   *   *   *   *   *   *   *   *

(d) Although indexed-sequential file design is not as easy to implement as standard sequential design, nor is access as fast as direct-access design, it has the advantage of permitting both direct access and sequential processing of the file.

9. The smallest unit of a record is a
    a. field   c. file
    b. data set   d. list

    *   *   *   *   *   *   *   *   *   *

(a) The smallest unit into which a record can be broken down into is a field. It is a single item, such as a name or a social security number.

10. Which of the following is not a capability of most data base management systems?
    a. provides for concurrent retrieval and updating of records
    b. writes application programs to access the data base
    c. integrates data into logical structures which represent actual relationships
    d. provides privacy controls to prevent unauthorized access

    *   *   *   *   *   *   *   *   *   *

(b) While a, c, and d are within the capability of most data base management systems, the application programs must be written by a skilled programmer familiar with the data base.

TRUE/FALSE

1.   T   F   Another name for a file is a record.

2.   T   F   A key is a field whose value will always be unique
             to a particular record.

3.   T   F   Data bases can cause a great deal of duplication of
             data.

4.   T   F   An index may also be referred to as a directory.

5.   T   F   Logical design refers to how data is stored in the
             computer's secondary storage devices.

6.   T   F   Another name for hashing is randomizing.

7.   T   F   When it is often necessary to locate a particular
             record in a file, sequential file processing is
             probably the most efficient method.

8.   T   F   Indexed-sequential design allows for both sequential
             processing and direct access.

9.   T   F   Sequential-access files are generally stored on
             disk.

10. T   F   When records are ordered in a specific sequence,
             this is referred to as linear structure.

MATCHING

a. hierarchical structure   f. magnetic disks
b. inverted structure   g. attributes
c. direct-access   h. list
d. record   i. data base management
e. updating   systems
                                 j. hashing

1.   _____ uses two files, a master file and a transaction
     file.

2.   When a record key is manipulated in such a way as to obtain
     a disk address, this is referred to as _____.

3.   A record in a data base is made up of fields, also called
      _____.

4.   A collection of related data items is a(n) _____.

5.   A group of records in which there is only one owner record
      and any number of member records is a(n) _____.

6.   A(n) _____ contains indexes for selected attributes in a
      file.

7.   Direct-access files must be stored on _____.

8.   A(n) _____ is a sequential arrangement of data records.

9.   _____ files can locate individual records quickly.

10.   _____ serve as interfaces between data bases and the data
      base users.

SHORT ANSWER

1.   Explain how sequential files are updated.

2.   When is it appropriate to use a sequential file design?

3.   Name two advantages of using a direct-access file.

4.   Why is it important that a key always uniquely identifies only one record?

5.   Give an example of a file that might contain records that are arranged in a hierarchical structure.

6.   Explain the terms activity and volatility.

7. Sometimes it is said that direct-access files do not "leave a trail." This refers to the fact that once a record is updated, the former record is lost. What problems can be caused by this?

8. What are two disadvantages of data bases?

9. Assume that you need to notify the university of an address change. If the university does not have a central data base, name some of the individual files that might need to be updated.

10. How does an inverted structure allow certain inquiries on a data base to be handled very quickly?

ANSWER KEY

True/False

1. F   3. F   5. F   7. F   9. F

Matching

1. e   3. g   5. a   7. f   9. c

Short Answer

1. Two files are used as input when updating a sequential file: the master file and the transaction file. As the two files are sequentially read, the key fields are checked to see if they match. If they do, the transaction record is copied to the new master file. Otherwise, the old master record is copied.

3. They allow individual records to be accessed quickly. They can allow several files to be updated concurrently.

5. A file on a student might contain an owner record listing the student's name, address, etc. and also a number of member records, each member record being a course in which the student is enrolled.

7. If there is a need to go back to the previous record, this is no longer possible since the record does not exist. This can create problems if a record is accidentally deleted or incorrectly updated.

9. Registrar's files, Bursar's files, the files in the college in which you are enrolled (such as Arts and Sciences).

Management Information and Decision Support Systems

KEY TERMS

Decision support system (DSS) – Information obtained from this system is used as a tool for managerial decision making.

Goal seeking – A form of simulation that allows the user to specify a desired result from which the values of the variables necessary to achieve the desired result are calculated by the DSS.

Management information system (MIS) – A formal network that extends computer use beyond routine reporting and into the area of management decision-making; the purpose of an MIS is to get the correct information to the appropriate manager at the right time.

Sensitivity analysis – A form of simulation that allows the user to identify the key variables within a decision support system model.

Simultaneous decision support system – A decision support system that attempts to incorporate into one system the decision making of various functional areas of an organization so that consistent, overall decisions can be made by management.

"What if" analysis – A form of simulation that allows the user to interactively process various decision alternatives to determine which one may be the best.

SUMMARY

A management information system (MIS) is a formal information network using computer capabilities to provide managers
with information necessary for making decisions. An MIS should
be designed so that it will provide reports that are decision-
oriented, results that the user needs, and expansion room for
future growth.

Three levels of management generally exist within an
organization and managers at each level require different types
of information. Top-level management requires information to
make strategic decisions regarding future activities of the
organization. Middle-level management requires information to
make tactical decisions related to the activities needed to
implement top-level strategies. Lower-level management needs
information in order to make daily operational decisions.

Management information systems should be designed to
generate several types of reports: scheduled listings, which
are produced at regular intervals and provide routine information to a wide variety of users; exception reports which alert
management to abnormal situations; predictive reports which aid
in planning; and demand reports which answer specific inquiries
requested by management.

Decision support systems (DSS), closely related to management information systems, provide information through computerized processes to help managers make relatively unstruc-
tured decisions.

The manager who will be using the DSS should develop a
model, based on the manager's own style and experience, which
represents how he or she views the situation. The DSS should,
then, be a unique decision tool tailored to fit the needs of the
manager. Simulation is a decision model designed to resemble a
real-world system. It allows the manager to experiment with
variables affecting the system. Sensitivity analysis, "what if"
analysis, and goal seeking are methods of simulation for which
managers can develop decision support systems.

A company's MIS must be structured to fit its information
needs and organizational structure. There are many possible
designs. A centralized design is set up to provide a common
data base for the entire organization. It permits economies of
scale, eliminates redundancy and duplication of data, and
results in efficient utilization of data-processing capability.

The hierarchical design segregates data along regional or functional lines. Each management level has the computer power necessary to support task objectives.

The distributed design is a variation of the centralized design. It permits the existence of independent operating units but recognizes the benefits of central coordination and control.

A decentralized design allows autonomous operating units the freedom to acquire their own hardware, develop software, and make personnel decisions independently.

STRUCTURED LEARNING

1.   Which of the following is not a characterisitic of a management information system?
     a.   has the capacity for expansion and future growth
     b.   produces decision-oriented results
     c.   generates reports that meet the user's needs
     d.   produces as much information as possible

     *   *   *   *   *   *   *   *   *   *

     (d)   Information overload is just as bad as too little information. With information overload, managers then face the problem of trying to distinguish what information is relevant and what is not.

2.   The level of decision-making that pertains to future-oriented activities is
     a.   strategic   c.   operational
     b.   tactical   d.   all of the above

     *   *   *   *   *   *   *   *   *   *

     (a)   The strategic planning and creative decision-making level emphasizes future-oriented activities such as establishing goals and determining strategies to achieve those goals.

3.   Preparing sales invoices would be an activity at what level of decision making?
     a.   strategic   c.   operational
     b.   tactical   d.   functional

     *   *   *   *   *   *   *   *   *   *

(c)   The operational decision-making level pertains to operating decisions made by first-line supervisors and foremen to ensure that specific jobs are done. Activities at this level include assigning jobs to workers, maintaining inventory records, and determining raw material requirements.

4.   An intermediate time horizon, a high use of internal information, and significant dependence on rapid processing and retrieval of data are characteristic of what level of decision-making?
a.   technical   c.   tactical
b.   operational   d.   strategic

    *   *   *   *   *   *   *   *   *   *

(c)   Tactical decision-making has a weekly/monthly time horizon, a high use of internal information, and a high reliance on online information. Decisions focus on determining the most efficient use of organization resources.

5.   The main problems in MIS design arise when determining the information requirements of which level of management?
a.   top-level
b.   middle-level
c.   lower-level
d.   It is equally hard to determine information requirements for all levels.

    *   *   *   *   *   *   *   *   *   *

(a)   Since most top-level management problems are nonrepetitive, have a great impact on the organization, and involve a great deal of uncertainty, it is extremely difficult to determine top-level information needs.

6.   Records that monitor performance and indicate deviations from expected results are
a.   demand reports   c.   scheduled listings
b.   predictive reports   d.   exception reports

    *   *   *   *   *   *   *   *   *   *

(d)   Exception reports are generated when deviations from usual performance results are indicated. They are useful because they focus management attention on situations which require special handling.

7.   The purpose of a DSS is to
     a.   support decisions made by managers
     b.   automate the manager's tasks
     c.   find the solution to a problem
     d.   replace management information systems

     *   *   *   *   *   *   *   *   *   *

     (a)   Information obtained from a DSS is used to support
     unstructured decisions. However, this does not mean that a
     DSS should replace an MIS, but rather supplement management
     information systems.

8.   The person(s) responsible for developing the models used in
     a DSS should be
     a.   top management in the company
     b.   a qualified system analyst
     c.   the manager using it
     d.   the operations manager

     *   *   *   *   *   *   *   *   *   *

     (c)   The manager who will be using the DSS should be the
     one to develop the model so that it represents the manager's
     perceptions of the situation. Management styles, environ-
     ments, experience, and judgments are unique to each manager
     and must be incorporated into a DSS designed to aid deci-
     sion making.

9.   The method of simulation that uses a decision support
     system to identify the key variables that warrant manage-
     ment's attention and then evaluates the effect any changes
     in the key variables would have on the outcome of a real
     world system is
     a.   modeling   c.   "what if" analysis
     b.   goal seeking   d.   sensitivity analysis

     *   *   *   *   *   *   *   *   *   *

     (d)   "What if" analysis allows a manager to interactively
     process a number of decision alternatives and quickly
     explore their outcomes. Goal seeking permits a manager to
     specify the desired outcome of a model, having the DSS pro-
     vide the required value of a variable needed to achieve
     that outcome.

10.   Which of the following is true of the centralized design
      approach of MIS structure?
      a.   A separate department is set up to provide data-
           processing facilities for the entire organization.
      b.   Each functional or geographic division has a central
           computer department.
      c.   Authority and responsibility for computer support are
           placed in autonomous organizational operating units.
      d.   both a and c

      *   *   *   *   *   *   *   *   *   *

      (a)   In a centralized approach, a separate EDP department
      is set up to provide data-processing facilities for the
      organization.   This department supports the operating units
      of the organization, is responsible for program development
      and hardware acquisition, and sets standard regulations and
      procedures to be followed by the entire organization.

TRUE/FALSE

1.   T   F   In a decentralized design approach, communication
               between units is limited or nonexistent, thereby
               ruling out the possibility of common, or shared,
               computer applications.

2.   T   F   In a decision support system, the computer can
               actually make its recommendation to the client.

3.   T   F   A frequent problem in the implementation of an MIS
               is determining what information is needed by each
               level of management.

4.   T   F   Predictive reports are used for anticipatory
               decision making (planning).

5.   T   F   Operational decision making is characterized by a
               daily time horizon.

6.   T   F   The success of an MIS depends mostly on the attitude
               and involvement of management.

7.   T   F   A system design may not incorporate features from
               both a hierarchical design and a distributed design.

8.   T   F   Much of the information in a scheduled listing
               report may not be relevant to a particular user.

9.   T   F   The system analyst should not rely on the user to
              determine the information requirement of an MIS.

10.   T   F   Commercial planning packages allow the manager to
              incorporate his or her own model of the system.

MATCHING

a. high   f. demand
b. decentralized   g. model
c. tactical   h. low
d. exception   i. simultaneous
e. decision-oriented   j. centralized

1.   _____ reports require the MIS to have an extensive and
well-structured data base to provide answers to unantici-
pated requests.

2.   An MIS must provide reports that are _____ .

3.   _____ decision making relates to implementing strategies
determined at the top level.

4.   Decisions made at the operational level require a(n)
_____ degree of judgment.

5.   _____ reports monitor the performance of a business and
alert management to abnormal situations.

6.   The heart of a decision support system is a(n) _____ .

7.   _____ decision support systems combine the various
interrelated functional areas of an organization into one
system.

8.   Decisions made at the strategic level require a(n) _____
degree of judgment.

9.   The most traditional design approach is the _____
approach.

10.   The _____ design approach is not highly compatible with
the management information system concept.

SHORT ANSWER

1.   What is the goal of a management information system?

2.   What are the advantages of a centralized design approach?

3.   What characteristics must an MIS have?

4.   List and explain the four types of reports an MIS can provide.

5.   How do decision support systems differ from management
     information systems?

6.   Explain the concept of corporate planning models or simul-
     taneous DSS.

7.   Give an example of when a distributed design approach to
     MIS might be used.

8.   Why might managers resist the use of an MIS?

9.   Why is a model the heart of a DSS?

10.   What is simulation?

ANSWER KEY

True/False

1. T   3. T   5. T   7. F   9. F

Matching

1. f   3. c   5. d   7. i   9. j

Short Answer

1.   The goal of an MIS is to get the correct information to the appropriate manager(s) at the right time.

3.   An MIS should provide decision-oriented reports, room for expansion and future growth, and results that users need.

5.   A DSS differs from an MIS by: 1) placing more emphasis on less structured decisions, 2) aiming toward effectiveness while the goal of MIS is efficiency, and 3) providing bene-fits to the strategic-level decision makers rather than the operational and tactical levels.

7.   The distributed design might be used to coordinate the
      activities of a large national chain store. Individual
      stores located in various cities across the nation need
      computer facilities at each store to keep track of sales,
      inventory, and personnel. But there still needs to be some
      central coordination of computer capabilities to con-
      solidate total company sales, inventory, and to control
      centralized operations such as catalog sales.

9.   In order for a DSS to provide managers with information
      that is helpful in making unstructured decisions, the
      manager must develop a model representing the real-world
      situation as he or she sees it. That model will incor-
      porate the variables the manager considers when making
      decisions without the help of a computer. Only from the
      model can a DSS get the right inputs which affect the out-
      put, according to a particular manager's perceptions.

16

The Impact of Computers on People and Organizations

KEY TERMS

Audio conferencing - A conference call that links three or more people.

Augmented audio conferencing - A form of teleconferencing that combines graphics and audio conferencing.

Bus network - A local area network in which multiple stations connected to a communication line can communicate directly with any other station on the line.

Computer-aided design (CAD) - The process of designing, drafting, and analyzing a prospective product using computer graphics on a video terminal.

Computer-aided manufacturing (CAM) - The process of using the computer to create a magnetic tape that will guide the machine tool in creating the particular part.

Computer anxiety - A fear individuals have of the effects computers have on their lives and society in general.

Computer conferencing - A form of teleconferencing that uses computer terminals for the transmission of messages; the participant need not be using the terminal in order to receive the message. It will be waiting the next time he or she uses the terminal.

Computer literacy - A broad, general knowledge of how to use computers to solve problems, of the functioning of the software and hardware, and an understanding of the societal implications of computers.

Computerphobia - See Computer anxiety.

Electronic mail - The transmission of messages at high speeds over telecommunication facilities.

Ergonomics - The method of researching and designing computer hardware and software to enhance employee productivity and comfort.

Facsimile systems - Produce a picture of a page by scanning it.

Local area network (LAN) - A specialized network that operates within a well-defined area, such as a building or complex of buildings, with the stations being linked by cable.

Network - The linking together of several CPUs.

Numerically controlled machinery - Manufacturing machinery that is driven by a magnetic punched tape created by a tape punch that is driven by computer software.

Office automation - The integration of computer and communication technology with traditional manual processes found in business offices.

Ring network - A classification of local area network in which multiple stations are each connected to adjacent stations; communication must be relayed through adjacent stations to the desired station.

Robotics - The science that deals with robots, their construction, capabilities, and applications.

Star network - A classification of a local area network in which multiple stations are connected to a central station; communication between stations must take place through the central station.

Telecommuting - Computer hookups between offices and homes, thereby allowing employees to work at home.

Telecomputing – A term referring to the use of online information services that offer access to one or more data bases; for example, CompuServe, The Source, and Dow Jones News/Retrieval.

Teleconferencing – The method of two or more remote locations communicating via electronic and image-producing facilities.

Telecopier systems – See Facsimile systems.

Teletypewriter systems – Transmit messages as strings of characters.

Video seminar – A form of teleconferencing that employs a one-way, full-motion video with two-way audio.

Videoconferencing – A technology that employs a two-way, full-motion video plus a two-way audio system for the purpose of conducting conferences between two remote locations through communication facilities.

Voice mail – See Voice message system.

Voice message system (VMS) – The sender activates a special "message" key on the telephone, dials the receiver's number, and records the message. A button lights on the receiver's phone, and when it is convenient, the receiver can activate the phone and listen to the message.

SUMMARY

The rush to computerize has caused some people to suffer computer anxiety, or computerphobia. Factors that may create high tech anxiety are a person's age and gender, computer jargon, exposure to computers, and fears of depersonalization.

Yet, people with no computer experience may be passed by for promotions and risk job insecurity. To combat this, schools are offering classes in computer literacy. Even adults must become computer-literate to compete in a high-tech world.

Job displacement and retraining are issues that must be dealt with as computer technology automates more jobs and processes. Retraining has helped many people; the skills and education required for many computer-related jobs differ from those required for the eliminated jobs.

Computerization has especially been evident in office functions--many of which are becoming automated. Almost every office function can be accomplished by computer. But workers must be considered, too. Ergonomics is the study and design of computer hardware, software, environment, and policies to increase the productivity, comfort, and safety of workers. Two primary areas for consideration are eyestrain and backstrain.

Two areas of office automation are word processing--the manipulation of text by computer--and office communications. Electronic mail helps offices with routine, internal com- munications. It involves sending messages at high speeds over telecommunication channels, and can be in the form of a tele- typewriter, facsimile, or voice message system.

Other communications benefit from teleconferencing tech- nology. The simplest form is the audio conference, which links three or more phones in conference. Other teleconferencing methods include the augmented audio conference, computer con- ference, video seminar, and videoconference.

Telecommuting is another computer practice that will affect our future work. More people will work at home on terminals and send material to the office by some type of telecommunication channel, probably leased telephone lines.

As more and more companies and individuals acquire com- puters, they will use telecomputing--the accessing of online information services or data bases for the latest in current events, financial information, sporting events, drugs, etc.

Many businesses also will be acquiring LANs, or Local Area Networks. LANs link computers in a small area, usually less than two miles, so users can share data, peripherals, and storage.

Computers have streamlined business operations in three major areas. The first is accounting and finance. Here general accounting software, the electronic spreadsheet, and data management software have eliminated much tedious paperwork. The second area, management, has used computers to provide a core of material for decision making. Evaluating data for marketing and sales is a third area in which computers have affected busi- nesses.

In industry, computers have provided the capability to simulate products and manufacturing before investments are made in materials, machinery, and manpower. The processes for this simulation are computer-aided design, computer-aided manufacturing, and a combination of the two, CAD/CAM.   Robots are also increasingly used in industry.

The federal government, the single largest user of computers, uses computers in simulation and modeling during military training and weather forecasting.   Also, three large federal organizations--the Library of Congress, FBI, and IRS--make use of computerized data bases.

STRUCTURED LEARNING

1.   Which factors can affect computer anxiety?
      a.   age
      b.   computer jargon
      c.   fear of depersonalization
      d.   all of the above

      *   *   *   *   *   *   *   *   *   *

(d) All of the factors can affect the attitudes of some people at some time.

2.   Computer literacy
      a.   has a standard definition used in all computer courses
      b.   means being able to take apart electronic equipment
      c.   means being able to read about computers
      d.   may affect one's marketability for many jobs

      *   *   *   *   *   *   *   *   *   *

(d) Computer literacy has no standard definition currently, so (a) is incorrect.   Some instructors may include knowledge about electronic equipment, but that is only part of computer literacy.   Therefore, (b) is not the best answer.   Being able to read may affect ability to learn, but again is not an encompassing definition of computer literacy.   But having computer literacy may affect one's ability to get a job and stay on that job in a world that is ever increasing in computer use.   So (d) is the best answer.

3.   Jobs that are lost to computers may be offset by
      a.   the growth of a company
      b.   the agricultural environment
      c.   word processing
      d.   office automation

      *   *   *   *   *   *   *   *   *   *

(a) A growing company may be able to find new positions for most of the employees whose jobs are taken over by computerized operations. On the other hand, word processing and office automation may simply displace more workers. The agricultural environment will not directly affect the jobs lost to computers.

4.   In order to make a smooth transition to computerized operations, managers would do well to consider
    a. ergonomics   c. robots
    b. popular programs   d. new products

    *   *   *   *   *   *   *   *   *   *

(a) Although b, c, and d may indirectly affect transitions to computers, the best answer is ergonomics. Ergonomics has to do with the comfort and productivity of the workers using the computers and computer environments.

5.   According to the text, how might color affect word processing in the future?
    a. It will keep the jobs of word processing personnel from becoming boring.
    b. It will make word processors more portable.
    c. It will code the revisions and identify the most recent revision.
    d. It will make voice input possible for word processors.

    *   *   *   *   *   *   *   *   *   *

(c) Color will not affect the portability of word processors or the possibility of voice input. Although it may make jobs more interesting, the text notes that color will enhance the revision process of preparing documents.

6.   Electronic mail systems do not
    a. allow the sender to cancel the message if it has not yet been read by the recipient
    b. require the recipients to be in the same building as the senders
    c. allow the "mail" to be printed out in hard copy
    d. allow senders to name a future date for delivering the "mail"

    *   *   *   *   *   *   *   *   *   *

(b) Recipients of electronic mail can be in remote locations to receive their "mail." However, various mail
systems do allow the options named in answers a, c, and d.

7.   The form of teleconferencing that requires the least amount
     of special equipment is
     a. videoconferencing   c. audio conferencing
     b. computer conferencing   d. video seminars

     *   *   *   *   *   *   *   *   *   *

(c) Audio conferencing is the lowest level of teleconferencing and requires the least sophisticated equipment.
The others all require special equipment, some of which is
beyond the budget of many companies.

8.   If you access the services of The Source, you are engaging
     in which function?
     a. telecommuting   c. telecomputing
     b. videoconferencing   d. voice mail

     *   *   *   *   *   *   *   *   *   *

(c) The Source provides access to data bases. Getting
access to a data base via computer is referred to as telecomputing. Telecommuting is a way to "get to the office"
without going to the office. Voice mail involves voice
messages, and videoconferencing is a process of running
televised face-to-face meetings via computers.

9.   A LAN allows user to
     a. share information, storage devices, and peripherals
     b. communicate over great distances with other CPUs
     c. provide a computing environment where little infor-
         mation needs to be shared among the company's person-
         nel
     d. share star, bus, and ring networks

     *   *   *   *   *   *   *   *   *   *

(a) A LAN is a local area network. Since the workstations
cannot be more than two miles apart, a LAN could not be
implemented over great distances. In answer c, changing
"little" to "much" would make the answer correct, since a
LAN provides a sharing environment. LANs come in different
types of networks--the star, bus, and ring. One office
would be apt to have only one type of network.

10.   A CAD/CAM environment
      a.   is an environment in which only managers are comfor-
           table
      b.   is an environment which costs more than it is worth,
           since it is not yet economical
      c.   is used only in the field of robotics
      d.   is a simulation environment

      *   *   *   *   *   *   *   *   *   *

(d) CAD/CAM is computer-aided design and manufacture. It
allows engineers to try out products and manufacturing
processes before they are actually implemented. This type
of simulation environment saves money for companies because
problems are spotted before expensive equipment and raw
materials are purchased or changed.

TRUE/FALSE

1.   T   F   Some factors which may contribute to high tech
                anxiety are a person's age, the jargon associated
                with computers, and the fear of depersonalization.

2.   T   F   Computer literacy courses in schools are important
                because students must know how to take apart circuit
                boards.

3.   T   F   The book implies that increased automation does not
                lead to increased unemployment.

4.   T   F   Two major complaints of workers using computers
                daily are eyestrain and backstrain.

5.   T   F   The field dealing with the comfort of workers using
                computers is called agronomics.

6.   T   F   Word processing is only one process that is included
                in the term office automation.

7.   T   F   Voice mail systems are no different from the stan-
                dard answering machines.

8.   T   F   Procuring the ability to hold audio conferences
                requires major equipment expenditures.

9.   T   F   Video conferencing is a cheap way to overcome the
                difficulties of audio conferencing.

10.   T   F   The types of communication media used in a LAN are star, bus, and ring.

MATCHING

a.   ergonomics   f.   word processing
b.   robotics   g.   VMS
c.   LAN   h.   CAM
d.   computerphobia   i.   facsimile system
e.   telecommuting   j.   network

1.   Controlling and/or simulating the manufacturing process by computer is accomplished by _____.

2.   The science of studying, constructing, and using the "new steel worker" is called _____.

3.   One can effect greater productivity in offices and greater employee comfort at computer workstations by applying the methods of _____.

4.   The process of manipulating text with a computer is called _____.

5.   Linking CPUs and terminals by a communication system is referred to by the generic term _____.

6.   The anxiety that some people exhibit toward using computers is called _____.

7.   A way to use the telephone to leave messages other than the standard answering machines is _____.

8.   Commuting to the office by means of computer is called _____.

9.   A network that can link workstations under two miles apart is called a _____.

10.   A system which will produce a picture of a page by copying it and sending it by electronic mail is called a _____.

SHORT ANSWER

1. Describe depersonalization as related to computer anxiety.

2. Why is computer literacy considered to be important?

3. What factors make a difference in the amount of job displacement when a transition to computers is made in a company?

4. Name two ways farmers might use microcomputers.

5.   List some functions of word processing.

6.   How does word processing make an office more efficient?

7.   Differentiate between voice message systems and standard
      answering machines.

8.   Why might a company choose augmented audio conferencing
      over audio conferencing or videoconferencing?

9. How can CAD/CAM save money for manufacturers?

10. How do data bases help the federal government manage its functions?

ANSWER KEY

True/False

1. T   3. T   5. F   7. F   9. F

Matching

1. h   3. a   5. j   7. g   9. c

Short Answer

1. People fear that using computers for such things as record keeping and billing leads to a feeling of being treated as a number rather than as a person.

3. A company might avoid job displacement if it uses computers so personnel can handle an increased workload, if it is a growing business, or if it anticipates personnel changes before computers are placed in the company.

5.   • automatic centering
      • reformatting of paragraphs
      • alphabetizing
      • pagination
      • justification of type
      • search and find
      • moving blocks of text

7.   In voice mail systems, the recipient can fast-scan the
      messages and the sender can send longer messages than are
      possible on answering machines.

9.   It allows the testing of products for stress points and
      part tolerance before a product is actually built. The
      manufacturing simulation can pinpoint major problems that
      might be encountered on the assembly line. CAM also
      records how tools are guided, so that information can be
      stored on magnetic tape for future use.

Computer Security, Crime, Ethics, and the Law

KEY TERMS

Breach of contract – The instance when goods fail to meet the terms of either an express or implied warranty.

Common law – Law that is based on customs and past judicial decisions in similar cases.

Computer crime – A criminal act that poses a greater threat to a computer user than it would a non-computer user, or a criminal act that is accomplished through the use of a computer.

Computer ethics – A term used to refer to the standard of moral conduct in computer use; a way in which the "spirit" of some laws are applied to computer-related activities.

Computer security – Instituting the technical and administrative safeguards necessary to protect a computer-based system against the hazards to which computer systems are exposed and to control access to information.

Decrypted – Data that are translated back into regular text after being encrypted for security reasons.

Encrypted – A term describing data that are translated into a secret code for security reasons.

Express warranties – Created when the seller makes any promise or statement of fact concerning the goods being sold which the purchaser uses as a basis for purchasing the goods.

Hacking – A term used to describe the activity of computer enthusiasts who are challenged by the practice of breaking computer security measures designed to prevent unauthorized access to a particular computer system.

Implied warranty – A warranty that provides for the automatic inclusion of certain warranties in a contract for the sale of goods.

Implied warranty of fitness – A situation where the purchaser relies on a seller's expertise to recommend a good that will meet his or her needs; if the good later fails to meet the purchaser's needs the seller has breached the warranty.

Implied warranty of merchantability – Guarantees the purchaser that the good purchased will function properly for a reasonable period of time.

Piracy – The unauthorized copying of a computer program written by someone else.

Privacy – An individual's right regarding the collection, processing, storage, dissemination, and use of data about personal attributes and activities.

Software copying – See Piracy.

Uniform Commercial Code (UCC) – A set of provisions proposed by legal experts to promote uniformity among state courts in the legal treatment of commercial transactions between sellers and purchasers.

SUMMARY

In a broad perspective, computer crime is defined as any criminal act that poses a greater threat to a computer user than it would to a non-computer user, or a criminal act that is accomplished through the use of a computer. The computer can be the target in two ways: as the instrument of committing the crime and as the "victim" of vandalism, theft, or demands for ransom. Four categories of computer crime are sabotage, theft of services, theft of property, and financial crimes.

However, computers are valuable in the prevention and detection of crime, too. They can help pinpoint arson targets, monitor people who are potential threats to public officials, and provide data bases containing information about murderers and other criminals. A major question arises, though, about the possibility of an innocent person's name finding its way into one of the data bases of those people who pose a threat to public officials.

Physical threats to computers are fire; natural disasters such as floods, hurricanes, and earthquakes; environmental problems such as bursting pipes, electrical problems, and magnetic fields; and sabotage--the greatest physical threat to computer systems.

Data security measures must be taken to prevent loss of data or unauthorized use. Passwords, internal security, limited access, encryption, and other measures can protect a system.

Computer ethics addresses the problem of moral or proper conduct about computer and software use. It is largely dependent upon human nature. Topics of ethics include hacking, piracy, security and privacy of data, and employee loyalty.

A particular problem is the use of data bases. Much of the data collected may not always be secure; the accuracy, completeness, and currency of the data may be low; decisions are made solely on the basis of those data; and much data are not needed for the purposes they were supposedly collected.

The Privacy Act of 1974 attempts to protect people whose records are in the hands of the federal government. It offers ways for people to correct wrong information, governs how the data may be used, tries to ensure the reliability of the data, and opens files so people can learn what data are being kept about them.

Warranties under the Uniform Commercial Code (UCC) address contract disputes. For the code to be applicable, the contract must be one for goods rather than services, and should be for the sales of goods, not for leases or licenses. Under Article Two, express warranties and implied warranties are created on behalf of the purchaser. The warranties protect the consumer concerning products bought upon promises of the seller, that is, certain warranties exist automatically merely by the making of a contract for the sale of goods.

Copyright law is a method of protecting computer programs from being pirated, but does not protect against unauthorized use of programs. Copyright registration is not required. However, if damages would ever be sought for a copyright infringement, registration would be necessary.

STRUCTURED LEARNING

1.   Computer crime is unique because
      a.   criminals can use the computer to cover the existence
           of the crime
      b.   criminals are geniuses
      c.   law officers can't arrest a computer
      d.   all of the above

      *   *   *   *   *   *   *   *   *

      (a) Not only can criminals use the computer to cover up the
      existence of the crime but they can use it to conceal their
      own identities.

2.   Few computer crimes are ever reported because
      a.   they are hushed up to avoid scaring customers and
           stockholders
      b.   company executives do not know enough about computers
           to detect them
      c.   law officers feel that solving computer crimes seems to
           depend on luck
      d.   all of the above

      *   *   *   *   *   *   *   *   *

      (d) All of these are reasons why so few computer crimes are
      reported to the police. Also because the complexity of
      data processing confuses the judicial system, few convic-
      tions and jail terms result.

3.   What presents the greatest risk to any computer installa-
      tion?
      a.   fire   c.   sabotage
      b.   fraud   d.   theft

      *   *   *   *   *   *   *   *   *

      (c) It is very difficult and expensive to provide adequate
      security against deliberate sabotage. Great damage can be
      done by sabotaging computer centers, with little risk of
      apprehension.

4.   One way to help secure data at a computer installation is to
   a.   grant access to only those whose jobs necessitate it
   b.   only allow the management to access the data bases
   c.   neglect to prosecute computer criminals so that out-siders will continue to believe the system is secure
   d.   locate the system in the basement of the building

   *   *   *   *   *   *   *   *   *

   (a) The other answers given would either decrease security or be unrealistic for workers who need access to the system.

5.   The loyalty of employees is of concern to companies today because
   a.   a considerable amount of job changing occurs among data-processing personnel
   b.   the Privacy Law of 1974 allowed employees to take any information they obtained while working for one company with them to a new job
   c.   most employees are involved in white-collar hacking
   d.   most employees have access to backup copies of data

   *   *   *   *   *   *   *   *   *

   (a) With the shortage of qualified personnel, data-processing people may frequently be offered jobs with other companies and therefore, may change jobs often to increase their chances of better salaries, etc.

6.   One of the main concerns of the privacy issue is
   a.   accuracy of the data
   b.   the banking sector
   c.   allowing institutions to operate more efficiently
   d.   the business sector

   *   *   *   *   *   *   *   *   *

   (a) The accuracy, completeness, and currency of the data may be unacceptably low.

7.   Which law was established to protect the privacy of indivi-
      duals whose files are maintained by the federal government?
      a.   Uniform Commercial Code (UCC)
      b.   the Common Law Enactment of 1978
      c.   the Privacy Act of 1974
      d.   Article Two

      *   *   *   *   *   *   *   *   *

      (c) This act also includes restrictions on the dissemina-
      tion of personal data by federal agencies.

8.   Computer vendors are liable for
      a.   hardware they sell
      b.   software they sell
      c.   nothing since the courts haven't decided yet
      d.   both a and b

      *   *   *   *   *   *   *   *   *

      (d) Vendors are liable for both the hardware and software
      that they sell. Also, software and hardware manufacturers
      have certain responsibilities concerning the performance of
      their products.

9.   The implied warranty of fitness guarantees that if equip-
      ment does not fill the needs of the buyer
      a.   all money will be returned
      b.   it will be replaced only if written agreements have
            been signed
      c.   the purchaser can recover only a certain amount of the
            sales price
      d.   the seller can recover only a certain amount of the
            sales price

      *   *   *   *   *   *   *   *   *

      (c) The buyer must communicate the purpose for which the
      products will be used. Then the supplier is liable for
      damages if he has not selected suitable computer hardware
      and software for the buyer's needs. However, the warranty
      permits the purchaser to recover only a certain amount of
      the sales price.

10. The copyright law protects
     a. original material only if a person decides to sue for
         copyright infringement
     b. against unauthorized use
     c. against use of unpublished programs
     d. against unauthorized copying

     *   *   *   *   *   *   *   *   *

     (d) The copyright law does not protect against unauthorized
     use, for example, if a program written in a magazine is
     copied.

TRUE/FALSE

1.   T F Americans are losing billions of dollars to high-
            technology crooks whose crimes go undetected and
            unpunished.

2.   T F The use of distributed systems decreases the oppor-
            tunities for computer crime and privacy violations.

3.   T F Computer crimes are often called "blue collar
            crimes."

4.   T F Computers may be targets of sabotage by political
            activists.

5.   T F The degree of damage to a computer system is
            directly proportional to the sophistication of the
            computer criminal.

6.   T F Fingerprints or voice patterns can provide one means
            of identifying legitimate computer users.

7.   T F One of the major problems associated with com-
            puterized data banks is the inability of the indivi-
            dual to control the personal data that is stored and
            disseminated about him or her.

8.   T F The use of the social security number as a common
            identifier in data banks greatly reduces the possi-
            bility that unauthorized people will get access to
            information about someone else.

9.   T F   One of the provisions of the Privacy Act of 1974 is
              that an individual has the right to destroy any
              information about himself or herself in a data bank.

10.   T F   Common law is based on past laws.

MATCHING

a. encryption   f. backup
b. piracy   g. hackers
c. Uniform Commercial Code   h. sabotage
    (UCC)   i. computer security
d. breach of contract   j. Privacy Act of 1974
e. registered

1.   A type of computer crime that has to do with vandalism of
      hardware and data is called _____.

2.   A set of provisions which attempts to aid in solving
      contract disputes is the _____.

3.   The technical and administrative safeguards needed to pro-
      tect a computer-based system against major hazards are
      achieved by establishing _____.

4.   One way to provide protection against loss of data and
      programs is to make _____ copies and store them in an
      alternate location.

5.   Scrambling data in a secret code before transmission or
      storage is called _____.

6.   Breaking copyrights and copy-protected disks to copy soft-
      ware is called _____.

7.   The major legislation which attempts to protect privacy on
      the federal level is the _____.

8.   When the merchandise fails to conform to the express
      warranty, the seller has committed a(n) _____.

9.   When someone wishes to sue for copyright infringement, a
      copyright must be _____.

10. According to this book, computer enthusiasts who are
     challenged to break computer security measures designed to
     prevent unauthorized access are called _____.

SHORT ANSWER

1. Name the two major ways a computer fits into criminal
    activities.

2. When computers are used in theft of property, why could the
    courts get tangled up in the question of what actually
    constitutes property?

3. Explain why the FBI's "crime predictor" is being criti-
    cized.

4.   If you were a systems analyst, what security measures would
      you recommend in light of the material presented about
      environmental problems for computer systems?

5.   What are two major objectives of using computers and how
      could excessive security requirements make a computer
      system less effective?

6.   If you were a manager or personnel director, what four com-
      pany policies and hiring and firing practices would you
      implement?

7.   Name the five major concerns about privacy.

8.   How does the Uniform Commercial Code (UCC) reflect an improvement over common law practices?

9.   What two conditions must be present for the UCC to apply to computer acquisitions?

10. How does the definition of express warranties protect the consumer?

ANSWER KEY

True/False

1. T   3. F   5. F   7. T   9. F

Matching

1. h   3. i   5. a   7. j   9. e

Short Answer

1.   The computer can be used to do acts of deceit, theft, or concealment that provide financial, business-related, property, or service advantages. The computer system itself can be the target of theft, vandalism, or threats of ransom.

3.   People worry that the Justice Department is using the system to monitor people who are considered a threat to officials but who have never really committed a crime.

5.   The two major objectives of using computers are economy and convenience. Many security measures, especially those using fingerprint or voice pattern identification, are very expensive. Some of these measures make a computer system less economical to use. The inconvenience of having to relocate backup copies, use codes, passwords, and special cards, encounter internal security forces each time you need to use the system, and constantly change passwords may bother people. Although security may seem exaggerated to some employees, management must decide how much is necessary in light of what information must be kept inaccessible to which employees.

7.   ● too much information being collected
     ● accuracy, completeness, and currency of information
     ● data irrelevant for purposes for which they will be used
     ● decisions made solely on basis of computerized records
     ● security of data

9.   The contract must be one for goods, not services, and it must be for sale of goods, not lease or license.

Computers in Our Lives: Today and Tomorrow

KEY TERMS

Artificial intelligence (AI) – A field of research currently developing techniques whereby computers can be used to solve problems that appear to require imagination, intuition, or intelligence.

Biomechanics – The application of engineering methodologies to biological systems.

Brain-wave interface – A technology that allows a user to control computer resources by using his or her brain wave patterns.

CADUCEUS – An artificial intelligence, expert system that diagnoses medical problems.

Computer modeling – The use of computers to model animal biological systems, for example, in place of the animals themselves; using computers to act as a real system for testing purposes.

Computer-assisted instruction (CAI) – Direct interaction between a computer and a student in which the computer serves as an instructor.

Computer-assisted diagnosis – A technique that allows the computer to compare numerical data gathered from a patient to normal or standard data in helping the physician to make a diagnosis.

Computerized tomography (CT or CAT) scanning – A form of computer-assisted diagnosis in which X-ray techniques are combined with computer technology to provide for quick and accurate physical diagnosis.

Data-base producers – Companies that compile and store huge, hard-copy data bases for use by online service companies.

Electron microscope tomography – The use of a computer and individual electrons to view microscopic biological material as a three-dimensional image.

Electron microscopy (EM) – The use of individual electrons to view microscopic material as a two-dimensional image.

Expert systems – A form of artificial intelligence in which the software is designed to program the computer to follow the same decision-making process as top experts in specific fields.

Multiphasic health testing (MPHT) – A form of computer-assisted diagnosis that compiles information on patients and their test results, which are compared to norms or means in order to aid the physician in making a diagnosis.

Nonmonotonic logic – The theory that logic should develop in steps, consistent with all preceding steps and that additional assumptions will not make the previous conclusions false.

Script theory – An approach to artificial intelligence that says that memories of a situation within our minds dictate how we, as humans, would think or act in a particular situation; (this is an attempt to apply this logic to developing computer intelligence).

SUMMARY

Computers will continue to have an impact on home life, education, entertainment, sports, the arts and sciences, and medicine. At the same time, scientists will be researching brain-wave interface and artificial intelligence, computer technologies of the future.

As people obtain computers for their homes, they will have the potential to shop and bank from home and access online data bases for current information. They also may acquire several microcomputers to manage their home's environment for efficient

energy use, security, fire prevention, and record-keeping needs.
Robots may appear more frequently in homes, although robot technology is still limited.

Young people and adults will learn about computers at
school and at camps. Students at school will also use computers
for CAI--computer-assisted instruction--in an unintimidating,
one-on-one atmosphere. Yet students who are using CAI in its
current form are not becoming computer literate, although they
may become more comfortable with using computers. In some
schools, computers are being combined with graphics, videodiscs,
and speech synthesizers to increase learning.

In medicine, application of computers in computer-assisted
diagnosis is evident in the use of computerized tomography (CT
or CAT) scanning, and multiphasic health testing (MPHT). Both
are tools which help physicians increase their effectiveness.
Hospitals are also using computerized life support to help
nurses to do a better job.

In science, computers decrease the time it takes for
complex mathematical calculations, classification of data, and
testing. Computer modeling helps scientists perform tests
through simulation, rather than actual animal tests. However,
using computer modeling procedures does not totally eliminate
the need for animal tests.

Artists, writers, and musicians use computers to produce
portraits and compositions, as well as edit their work.
Athletes can use computers to help improve the form of their
movements. And tourists can gain insight into modern technology
by touring such futuristic displays as EPCOT Center in Florida.

Two new technologies which are being explored are brain-
wave interface and artificial intelligence. Brain-wave interface involves controlling a computer with brain response, while
artificial intelligence involves imitating the thought and
reasoning abilities of humans.

STRUCTURED LEARNING

1. In the future, homeowners may use computers to
    a. shop
    b. complete banking transactions
    c. control the home environment
    d. all of the above

    *   *   *   *   *   *   *   *   *

    (d) All are true.

2. Online data bases have
    a. proven very popular
    b. declined in growth since 1979
    c. provided 24-hour banking
    d. contributed to the decline in purchasing of home com-
        puters

    *   *   *   *   *   *   *   *   *

    (a) Online data bases grew from 59 listings in the
    Directory of Online Data Bases in 1979 to 213 listings in
    1982.

3. Computer-assisted instruction (CAI) allows students to
    a. miss school
    b. progress through lessons at their own pace
    c. completely achieve computer literacy
    d. attend camp

    *   *   *   *   *   *   *   *   *

    (b) Computer-assisted instruction guides students through
    material, but does not make a student computer-literate or
    permit missing school or attending camp.

4. Some CAI combines use of computers and
    a. speech synthesizers   c. graphics
    b. videodiscs   d. all of the above

    *   *   *   *   *   *   *   *   *

    (d) All of the technologies listed have been used with com-
    puters in schools.

5.   Computer-assisted diagnosis includes
      a.   CAT scanning   c.   UCC
      b.   MPHT   d.   a and b

      *   *   *   *   *   *   *   *   *

      (d) Answer c is incorrect because UCC has to do with
      contract disputes.

6.   Computerized monitoring systems provide an advantage to
      hospitals because
      a.   constant bedside nursing is required
      b.   information on as many as eight patients can be
           displayed at a nursing station
      c.   critically ill people need CAT scans
      d.   the computer will take care of any emergencies

      *   *   *   *   *   *   *   *   *

      (b) Nurses can watch several patients at once, and an alarm
      will sound from the computer if something goes wrong with
      one particular patient.

7.   Computer modeling in biology laboratories will enable
      scientists to
      a.   use more animals for testing drugs and chemicals
      b.   simulate by computer human and animal biological func-
           tions, which should decrease the number of animals used
           in biological experimentation
      c.   use special glasses to view images
      d.   monitor as many as eight patients

      *   *   *   *   *   *   *   *   *

      (b) Computer modeling will help scientists imitate biologi-
      cal functions by computer, which will save on the number of
      animals used in tests. Answers c and d have to do with
      other processes.

8.   At the COTO Research Center biomechanics is helping people
      to
      a.   use videodiscs with computers
      b.   learn how to make mechanical drawings
      c.   learn how to use digitizers
      d.   improve their form while engaging in athletic movements

      *   *   *   *   *   *   *   *   *

(d) The science of biomechanics involves the use of high-speed cameras, digitizer pens, computers, and computer software in the process of analyzing movement.

9.   Brain-wave interface will enable a person to
    a.   eliminate interference of neck muscle contractions
    b.   control a computer by brain waves which respond to light stimuli in distinct patterns
    c.   learn artificial intelligence
    d.   learn script theory thinking

    *   *   *   *   *   *   *   *   *

(b) A person wears electrodes like those used for an electroencephalogram and gazes at a flashing light chosen from a board of lights, each representing an action or data item. By responding to the different flash patterns the person looks at, the brain controls the computer.

10.   Two concepts which may help in development of artificial intelligence are
    a.   CAT and CAI
    b.   CADUCEUS and expert systems
    c.   nonmonotonic logic and script theory
    d.   script theory and CommuniCore

    *   *   *   *   *   *   *   *   *

(c) These two concepts help scientists envision how humans apply common sense, a difficult idea to program into artificial intelligence.

TRUE/FALSE

1.   T   F   The effects of computer technology on our lives have peaked and will decline in the future.

2.   T   F   The use of home computers for banking and shopping has met some resistance.

3.   T   F   Using online data bases can aid research.

4.   T   F   Computers can help homeowners make the best use of energy and reduce utility bills.

5.   T   F   The primary objective of computer literacy in the schools is for students to learn CAI.

6.   T   F   According to the text, most applications of computers in medicine are found in hospitals.

7.   T   F   Hospitals that want CAT scan techniques can save on costs by linking their scanning equipment to a central computer instead of purchasing their own computers.

8.   T   F   Computer modeling is expected to fully replace the use of live animals in laboratory research.

9.   T   F   Nonmonotonic logic may help in the development of artificial intelligence.

10. T   F   No expert systems are currently available, although packages will be available in the early 1990s.

MATCHING

a. environment
b. biomechanics
c. expert system
d. data-base producers
e. monitoring

f. three-dimensional
g. script theory
h. laser videodisc
i. multiphasic health testing (MPHT)
j. computer-assisted instruction (CAI)

1.   _____ compile data to sell to online services companies for home data base access.

2.   A computer-controlled home might have microcomputers which control its _____ .

3.   A student can interact with a computer to build skills and learn new material in the process known as _____ .

4.   A complete physical examination can be evaluated by computer during the process of _____ .

5.   In hospitals, computers can help with the _____ of patients.

6.   Although electron microscopy has been in use for nearly 25 years, it can be used in conjunction with computers to produce _____ images.

7.   Analyzing human movement using engineering techniques and computers is called _____.

8.   Worldkey Information Service integrates the technology of _____ to bring information to guests at CommuniCore at EPCOT Center.

9.   CADUCEUS is an example of a(n) _____.

10.   One approach toward designing artificial intelligence systems is _____.

SHORT ANSWER

1.   List some advantages of shopping by computer.

2.   Name some home functions that a computer could control.

3.   Explain how a CAI atmosphere can be unintimidating.

4.   Judging from the section in the text about MPHT, how does
     MPHT free a physician for higher quality patient inter-
     action?

5.   What is new about electron microscopy since computers have
     been combined with that technology?

6.   How might a musician use a computer?

7.   Using the information on biomechanics, how could the
     science of biomechanics be used in motion analysis of race
     horses?

8.   Name some technologies that WorldKey Information Service
      integrates to provide information to users.

9.   What is the current problem with brain-wave interface?

10.   What do expert systems do?

ANSWER KEY

True/False

1. F   3. T   5. F   7. T   9. T

Matching

1. d   3. j   5. e   7. b   9. c

Short Answer

1. ● avoid cost of driving
   ● avoid traffic
   ● avoid impulse buying
   ● feel safe from muggers

3. A student learns at his or her own pace by a patient "teacher" that can repeat instructions or processes as often as the student needs them.

5. Combined with computers, electron microscopy can now provide three-dimensional structures of biological material.

7. High-speed cameras would take pictures of a horse's running form. The film is used with a digitizer pen to enter the motions into the computer. Then computer software is used to analyze and evaluate the motion. Perhaps the output of various racing horses' forms could be analyzed for common factors of winning horses.

9. Brain-wave interface is still very slow, as computer speeds are measured.

BASIC
Supplement

SECTION I
Introduction to BASIC

STRUCTURED LEARNING

1. Which of the following is true of BASIC?
    a. BASIC is unpopular because of its lack of interactive
        capability.
    b. BASIC is short for Beginner's All-purpose Symbolic
        Instruction Code.
    c. BASIC is a programming language that has no syntax
        rules.
    d. BASIC was developed in the mid-1950s at Dartmouth
        College.

    *   *   *   *   *   *   *   *   *   *

    (b) BASIC is a programming language developed in the
    mid-1960s. It is popular because of its interactive capa-
    bilities, and it does contain rules for spelling, syntax,
    grammar, and punctuation.

2. The first step of the programming process is
    a. designing the program
    b. writing the program
    c. compiling, debugging, and testing the program
    d. defining the problem

    *   *   *   *   *   *   *   *   *   *

d)   The first step of the programming process is defining the problem.   Then, the solution can be designed, program written, and compiled, debugged, and tested.

3.   The flowchart symbol for a processing step is
a.   c.

b.   d.

*   *   *   *   *   *   *   *   *   *

(c)   is used for an input or output step; a   shows where the program starts or stops;   is used to show where a decision is to be made.

4.   The series of steps that enables us to produce the desired output from the available input is called
a.   the programming process   c.   an algorithm
b.   syntax   d.   documentation

*   *   *   *   *   *   *   *   *   *

(c) Syntax refers to the grammar and punctuation of the programming language; documentation is used to explain the program; an algorithm is developed in the first step of the programming process.

5.   _____   are used by the programmer to communicate with the operating system of the computer.
a.   system commands   c.   BASIC commands
b.   ANSI commands   d.   SYS commands

*   *   *   *   *   *   *   *   *   *

(a) System commands enable the programmer to communicate with the operating system to perform functions such as saving a program.

6. The LIST command
    a. displays a list of the file names in storage
    b. displays the program currently in primary memory
    c. moves the program in primary memory to secondary
        storage
    d. moves the requested program from secondary storage to
        primary memory

    *   *   *   *   *   *   *   *   *   *

    (a) The system command LIST displays the program that is
    currently in primary memory.

7. The LOAD command
    a. tells the computer to erase any program currently in
        active memory
    b. tells the computer to execute the program in primary
        memory
    c. tells the computer to move the program currently in
        primary memory to secondary storage
    d. tells the computer to move the designated program from
        secondary storage to primary memory

    *   *   *   *   *   *   *   *   *   *

    (d) The LOAD command is a system command that LOADs a
    specified program from a secondary storage device into
    primary memory.

8. The _____ command tells the computer to move the program
    currently in primary memory to secondary storage.
    a. LOAD   c. NEW
    b. SAVE   d. LIST

    *   *   *   *   *   *   *   *   *   *

    (b) The SAVE command is a system command used to move a
    program from primary storage to secondary storage so that
    the program is saved and can be used at a later time.

SECTION II
BASIC Fundamentals

STRUCTURED LEARNING

1. Which of the following is not true of line numbers?
    a. They must be positive integer values.
    b. Line numbers specify the order of execution of BASIC
        statements.
    c. Line numbers must be in increments of 1.
    d. Line numbers can be used as labels to refer to specific
        statements in a program.

    *   *   *   *   *   *   *   *   *   *

    (c) Line numbers can follow any size increment as long as
    they are positive integers between 1 and the upper limit of
    the computer. Line numbers are used both as labels and to
    indicate the order of execution of BASIC statements.

2. Constants
    a. are values that do not change during a program's execu-
        tion
    b. are only numeric values
    c. change their value throughout the program's execution
    d. may not be in exponential notation

    *   *   *   *   *   *   *   *   *   *

(a) Constants may be numeric or character string values that do not change during a program's execution.

3. Which of the following is true of exponential notation?
    a. It is never used with very large or small numbers.
    b. The "E" represents the power to which 10 is raised.
    c. The signed number following the "E" is the mantissa.
    d. The plus sign (+) indicates the decimal point is to be shifted to the right.

*   *   *   *   *   *   *   *   *   *

(d) The plus sign (+) indicates the decimal point is to be shifted to the right the power number of places and the minus sign (-) indicates it is to be shifted left.

4. Which of the following is not a valid numeric variable name?
    a. X1   c. Q4
    b. Z   d. 9J

*   *   *   *   *   *   *   *   *   *

(d) According the the ANSI standard, a numeric variable name can be either one letter alone or one letter followed by a single digit.

5. Which of the following is a valid string variable name?
    a. F$ c. $Z
    b. $6   d. 7$

*   *   *   *   *   *   *   *   *   *

(a) The ANSI standard indicates that a string variable consists of a single alphabetic character followed by a dollar sign ($).

WORKSHEET

1. Explain what a BASIC statement is and what it consists of.

2. Explain the difference between a constant and a variable.

3.   Convert the following numbers to exponential notation.
      Identify the power and mantissa of each.
      -5004.2
      .000329
      40762.17

4.   Identify the invalid variable names. Tell why they are
      invalid and change them to make them valid.
      a. 8$ d. 7F
      b. $X   e. Q$
      c. F   f. 3A$

5.   What are variable names? Explain the differences between
      the two types and what each represents.

6.   What are reserved words?

ANSWER KEY

Worksheet

1.   A BASIC statement tells the computer what operations to
      perform. It consists of special programming commands,
      numeric or character-string constants, numeric or string
      variables, and formulas or expressions.

3.
	Mantissa	Power
-5.0042E+03	-5.0042	+03
3.29E-04	3.29	-04
4.076217E+04	4.076217	+04

5.   Variable names are programmer-supplied names that specify
      locations in storage where data values (variables) may be
      stored. Numeric variable names represnt locations where
      numeric values may be stored. String variable names must
      end with a dollar sign and represent locations in storage
      where alphanumeric values are stored.

SECTION III
Getting Started with BASIC Programming

STRUCTURED LEARNING

1. Which of the following BASIC statements is a non-executable
    statement?
    a. LET
    b. END
    c. PRINT
    d. REM

    *   *   *   *   *   *   *   *   *   *

    (d) The REM statement is not executed by the computer. It
    is used to document the program for the programmer's use.

2. The LET statement
    a. assigns values to numeric variables only
    b. assigns values to numeric or string variables
    c. is used to print letters
    d. is used to document the program

    *   *   *   *   *   *   *   *   *   *

    (b) The LET statement assigns the value or result of a
    calculation on the right of the equal sign to the numeric
    or string variable on the left of the equal sign.

3.   What operation will be performed first in the following
      equation?
           A + 3 * (7/2 ∧ 3)
      a.   A + 3   c.   7/2
      b.   3 * 7   d.   2 ∧ 3

      *   *   *   *   *   *   *   *   *   *

      (d) 2 ∧ 3 will be done first because exponentiation has the
      highest priority.

4.   When assigning character strings to a string variable name,
      a.   the character string must be enclosed within quotation
           marks
      b.   the string variable name must appear on the right side
           of the equal sign
      c.   the PRINT statement should be used
      d.   a string variable name may never appear on the right
           side of the equal sign

      *   *   *   *   *   *   *   *   *   *

      (a) Character strings must be enclosed within quotation
      marks.   The value of a string variable name on the right of
      the equal sign may be assigned to a string variable name on
      the left.

5.   Which of the following is not true of the PRINT statement?
      a.   Literals may be used in a PRINT statement.
      b.   Variables in the PRINT statement are separated by
           commas.
      c.   When the PRINT statement is used to print variables it
           erases the value from storage.
      d.   The value of an arithmetic expression can be printed
           using the PRINT statement.

      *   *   *   *   *   *   *   *   *   *

      (c) The PRINT statement has no effect on the contents of
      storage.

WORKSHEET

1. What does the END statement do? On which line number of
    the program is it found? Give the general format for the
    END statement.

2. Excluding parentheses, give the priority of operations.
    Are the operations with highest or lowest priority per-
    formed first?

3. If two or more operations of the same priority appear in an
    equation, which is performed first?

4. What is the result of the following mathematical
    expressions?
    a.   T * (2 + 3) / S ∧ 3   where T = 8 and S = 2
    b.   C * D / 2 ∧ 4 * 9   where C = 6 and D = 8
    c.   X + Y * (Z / 4 + 6)   where X = 4, Y = 3, and Z = 20

5. Write a BASIC statement to assign the result of the
    following equations to a variable.

    a. $\dfrac{5 + 6}{9(.25)}$

    c. $\dfrac{Z^9 \ (.5)}{(Z + X) \div 2}$

    b. $\dfrac{7 \times 2^3}{B \div C}$

    d. $\dfrac{3 \div 4 + 2}{X + 3(\frac{1}{2})}$

6. Which of the following LET statements are invalid? Why?
    a.   20   LET S = "TRACEY MILLER"
    b.   30   LET 3.895 = X
    c.   40   LET Z$ = JANUARY

7. How can blank lines be printed? Write a statement(s) to
    print two blank lines.

8. Which of the following PRINT statements are invalid?
    Correct them.
    a.   10   PRINT "AGE IS",21   d.   40   "JANUARY NINTH"
    b.   20   PRINT "BIRTHDAY   e.   50   PRINT I = 90
    c.   30   PRINT   f.   60   PRINT 99, DOMINOS

9.   What will be PRINTED by the following program?
          10   LET S = 84
          20   LET T = 4
          30   LET X = S / (T / 2) + 10
          40   PRINT X
          50   PRINT "CARDS"

10.   For what is the REM statement used?   Why is it necessary?

PROGRAMMING PROBLEM 1

Auto Parts, Inc. sells spark plugs, gaskets, and batteries. On the average, 12 percent of the spark plugs, 10 percent of the gaskets, and 7.5 percent of the batteries are defective. Auto Parts has just completed inventory. There are 7,500 spark plugs 10,000 gaskets, and 300 batteries on hand.

The purchasing agent of Auto Parts wants a report listing the part, the approximate number of good parts, the approximate number of defective parts, and the total number of parts on hand.

The output should appear as follows:

PART	GOOD	DEFECTIVE	TOTAL
XXXXXXX	######	######	#######

PROGRAMMING PROBLEM 1 cont.

PROGRAMMING PROBLEM 2

You have been asked by the Way-Sales Computer Company to determine the highest selling computer during its annual Computer Bargain Sale. Following is a list of the computers, the number on hand at the beginning of the sale, and the number on hand after the sale:

COMPUTER	BEGINNING	END
Apple IIc	35	15
Apple IIe	15	5
Apple Macintosh	50	9
IBM-PC	30	11
IBM-PCjr	25	15
PET COMMODORE 64	15	7

Write a program to compute the percentage sold of each computer during the sale. Use the following output:

COMPUTER	PERCENTAGE
XXXXXXXXXX	XX
XXXXXXXXXX	XX
XXXXXXXXXX	XX

PROGRAMMING PROBLEM 2 cont.

ANSWER KEY

Worksheet

1.   The END statement indicates to the computer that the end of
      the program has been reached; therefore, it must have the
      highest line number in the program. Its general format is:
      line# END

3.   The operation in parentheses or, if there are no
      parentheses, the computer starts on the left and works to
      the right.

5.   a.   10 LET R = (5 + 6) / (9 * .25)
      b.   20 LET S = (7 * 2∧3) / (B / C)
      c.   30 LET Q = (Z∧9 * .5) / ((Z + X) / 2)
      d.   40 LET Y = (3 / 4 + 2) / (X + 3 * (1 / 2))

7.   A blank line is printed using a PRINT statement with
      nothing typed after it.
            10 PRINT
            20 PRINT

9.   52
      CARDS

PROGRAMMING PROBLEM 1

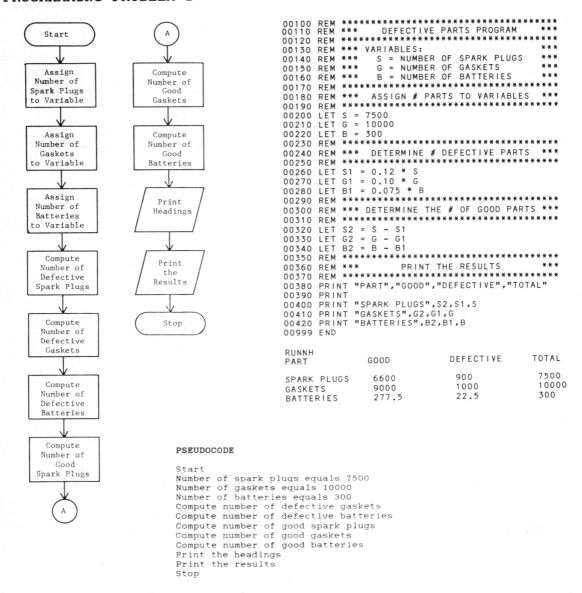

```
00100 REM ****************************************
00110 REM ***      DEFECTIVE PARTS PROGRAM      ***
00120 REM ****************************************
00130 REM *** VARIABLES:                        ***
00140 REM ***     S = NUMBER OF SPARK PLUGS     ***
00150 REM ***     G = NUMBER OF GASKETS         ***
00160 REM ***     B = NUMBER OF BATTERIES       ***
00170 REM ****************************************
00180 REM ***   ASSIGN # PARTS TO VARIABLES     ***
00190 REM ****************************************
00200 LET S = 7500
00210 LET G = 10000
00220 LET B = 300
00230 REM ****************************************
00240 REM ***    DETERMINE # DEFECTIVE PARTS    ***
00250 REM ****************************************
00260 LET S1 = 0.12 * S
00270 LET G1 = 0.10 * G
00280 LET B1 = 0.075 * B
00290 REM ****************************************
00300 REM *** DETERMINE THE # OF GOOD PARTS ***
00310 REM ****************************************
00320 LET S2 = S - S1
00330 LET G2 = G - G1
00340 LET B2 = B - B1
00350 REM ****************************************
00360 REM ***         PRINT THE RESULTS         ***
00370 REM ****************************************
00380 PRINT "PART","GOOD","DEFECTIVE","TOTAL"
00390 PRINT
00400 PRINT "SPARK PLUGS",S2,S1,S
00410 PRINT "GASKETS",G2,G1,G
00420 PRINT "BATTERIES",B2,B1,B
00999 END
```

RUNNH

PART	GOOD	DEFECTIVE	TOTAL
SPARK PLUGS	6600	900	7500
GASKETS	9000	1000	10000
BATTERIES	277.5	22.5	300

PSEUDOCODE

```
Start
Number of spark plugs equals 7500
Number of gaskets equals 10000
Number of batteries equals 300
Compute number of defective gaskets
Compute number of defective batteries
Compute number of good spark plugs
Compute number of good gaskets
Compute number of good batteries
Print the headings
Print the results
Stop
```

MICROCOMPUTERS

Apple	Output must be reformatted: no space is left for sign
Apple Macintosh	No space is left for sign
IBM/Microsoft	No differences
PET/Commodore 64	Output must be reformatted
TRS-80	No differences

SECTION IV
Input and Output

STRUCTURED LEARNING

1. The _____ statement allows data to be entered while a program is running.
   a. READ
   b. DATA
   c. INPUT
   d. LET

   *   *   *   *   *   *   *   *   *   *

   (c) The INPUT statement allows the user to enter data from the terminal while the program is running. This creates a question-and-answer, or inquiry-and-response, mode.

2. Which of the following is not true of the READ statement?
   a. The READ statement should be used with a prompt.
   b. The READ statement is used in conjunction with the DATA statement.
   c. READ statements are useful when large amounts of unchanging data are to be used.
   d. READ statements are located in a program wherever the logic of the program indicates the need for data.

   *   *   *   *   *   *   *   *   *   *

   (a) The READ statement is used when large amounts of unchanging data are to be input. Because it takes values from the data list, prompts are not necessary to explain to the user what data is to be entered.

3.   The comma, when used in PRINT statements, directs the com-
      puter to
      a.   space to the next print zone
      b.   space to the next column
      c.   start printing on the next line
      d.   The comma is not used in the PRINT statement.

      *   *   *   *   *   *   *   *   *   *

      (a) The comma is used to separate values in a PRINT state-
      ment. It directs the computer to space over to the next
      print zone before printing the next value.

4.   When the semicolon is used to separate values in the PRINT
      statement it causes the computer to
      a.   space to the next print zone
      b.   space to the next column
      c.   advance to the next line
      d.   backspace to the previous column

      *   *   *   *   *   *   *   *   *   *

      (b) The semicolon as used in the PRINT statement causes the
      computer to space to the next column to begin printing the
      next value.

WORKSHEET

1.   The statement that allows user interaction with the com-
      puter is _____ .

2.   Explain prompt. Give examples of the two methods of
      creating a prompt.

3.   What are the three methods of data entry? Explain when
      each is best used.

4.   What values will be assigned to the variables in the
      following READ statements?
      10   READ X,Y
      20   READ Z$,A
      30   DATA 9
      40   DATA 10,JASON,-393

5. Which of the following PRINT statements contain errors?
    Correct those errors.
    a.   10 PRINT "NAME" "I.D. NUMBER" "OCCUPATION"
    b.   20 PRINT X:Y:Z$
    c.   30 PRINT "DARREN",,"ASTRE";
    d.   40 PRINT "THE DATE IS;D$
    e.   50 "PRINT LICENSE NUMBER";L
    f.   60 PRINT A;B;C,

6. The following values must be stored in different variables.
    Show three different ways that this can be accomplished.
        CHAIRS, 8, TABLES, 2

7. When the following program is executed, in what columns
    will the headings begin?
        10 PRINT TAB(5);"EVENT"; TAB(20);"TIME"
        20 PRINT TAB(5);"-----"; TAB(20);"-----"

8. The _____ statement is a method of controlling output by
    avoiding print zone restrictions and "dressing up: the out-
    put.

9. Give the general format of the PRINT USING statement (and
    the image statement if it is used) for the computer(s) that
    you have been using.

10. Which of the following program segments will give the same
    output?
    a.   10 READ W,X,Y,Z   c.   10 READ W,X,Y,Z
         20 LET S = W + X + Y + Z   20 READ Y
         30 PRINT S   30 PRINT W + X + Y + Z
         40 DATA 9,10,-3,2,0   40 DATA 9,10
                                           50 DATA -3,2,0

    b.   10 READ W,X   d.   10 READ W,X,Y
         20 READ Y,Z   20 READ Z
         30 PRINT W + X + Y + Z   30 LET S = W + X + Y + Z
         40 DATA 9,10,-3,2,0   40 PRINT S
                                           50 DATA 9,10
                                           60 DATA -3,2

PROGRAMMING PROBLEM 1

A major department store wants you to write a program to enter a customer's purchase and form of payment using INPUT statements. Also, the store wants you to print out what you have entered to make sure the information is correct. The bills of sales are outlined below:

```
Karl Paglia              cash
Karla Simmons            credit
Steve Girnus             check
Tamara Vanderwall        credit
```

Write a program using the INPUT statements and prompts in an appropriate format.

PROGRAMMING PROBLEM 1 cont.

PROGRAMMING PROBLEM 2

The Census Bureau has asked you to write a program which will print a report consisting of the name of the household and the number of people residing in the house. At the end of the report, the Census Bureau wants a total of the number of people included in the report. The output should look as follows:

<pre>
              CENSUS BUREAU REPORT

        NAME   # RESIDENTS

        XXXXXXXXXXXXXXXX   ##
        XXXXXXXXXXXXXXXX   ##
        XXXXXXXXXXXXXXXX   ##
        XXXXXXXXXXXXXXXX   ##

        TOTAL: ###
</pre>

The input for the report is shown below:

<pre>
        NAME   # RESIDENTS

        Douglas   4
        Morgan   8
        Owens   11
        Sergisson   2
</pre>

PROGRAMMING PROBLEM 2 cont.

ANSWER KEY

Worksheet

1.   The INPUT statement allows interaction with the computer.

3.   The LET, INPUT, and READ/DATA statements are three methods
      of data entry. The LET statement should be used when there
      is a small amount of constant data to be used by the
      program, and also to initialize variables. The INPUT
      statement is used when an inquiry-and-response mode is
      desired, or where the data to be used in the program
      changes often. Use the READ/DATA statements to enter large
      amounts of unchanging data.

5.   a.   10 PRINT "NAME","I.D. NUMBER","OCCUPATION"
      b.   20 PRINT X;4;Z$
      c.   This statement is correct. PRINT statements may end
           with a semicolon.
      d.   40 PRINT "THE DATE IS";D$
      e.   50 PRINT "LICENSE NUMBER";L
      f.   This statement is correct. PRINT statements may also
           end with a comma.

7.   EVENT will begin in column 6
      and TIME will begin in column 21.

9.   DECSYSTEM 20:   line# PRINT USING image statement line#,
                          expression list
                      line#:   format control characters
      IBM/MICROSOFT and TRS-80:   line# PRINT USING "format";
                          expression list

PROGRAMMING PROBLEM 1

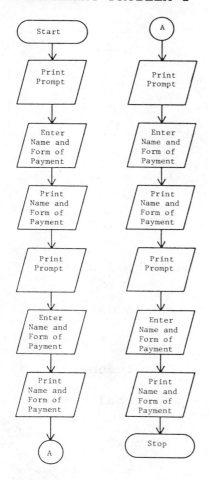

```
00100 REM *******************************
00110 REM *** PURCHASE INPUT PROGRAM ***
00120 REM *******************************
00130 REM *** VARIABLES:              ***
00140 REM ***    N$ = CUSTOMER'S NAME ***
00150 REM ***    P$ = FORM OF PAYMENT ***
00160 REM *******************************
00170 REM ***   ENTER AND PRINT NAME   ***
00180 REM ***     AND FORM OF PAYMENT  ***
00190 REM ***     FOR FOUR CUSTOMERS   ***
00200 REM *******************************
00210 PRINT "ENTER NAME AND FORM OF PAYMENT"
00220 INPUT N$,P$
00230 PRINT
00240 PRINT N$,P$
00250 PRINT
00260 PRINT "ENTER NAME AND FORM OF PAYMENT"
00270 INPUT N$,P$
00280 PRINT
00290 PRINT N$,P$
00300 PRINT
00310 PRINT "ENTER NAME AND FORM OF PAYMENT"
00320 INPUT N$,P$
00330 PRINT
00340 PRINT N$,P$
00350 PRINT
00360 PRINT "ENTER NAME AND FORM OF PAYMENT"
00370 INPUT N$,P$
00380 PRINT
00390 PRINT N$,P$
00999 END


RUNNH
ENTER NAME AND FORM OF PAYMENT
? KARL PAGLIA,CASH

KARL PAGLIA    CASH

ENTER NAME AND FORM OF PAYMENT
? KARLA SIMMONS,CREDIT

KARLA SIMMONS CREDIT

ENTER NAME AND FORM OF PAYMENT
? STEVE GIRNUS,CHECK

STEVE GIRNUS  CHECK

ENTER NAME AND FORM OF PAYMENT
? TAMMY VANDER

TAMMY VANDER  CREDIT
```

PSEUDOCODE

```
Start
Print prompt
Input name and form of payment
Print name and form of payment
Print prompt
Input name and form of payment
Print name and form of payment
Print prompt
Input name and form of payment
Print name and form of payment
Print prompt
Input name and form of payment
Print name and form of payment
Stop
```

MICROCOMPUTERS	
Apple	No differences
Apple Macintosh	No differences
IBM/Microsoft	No differences
PET/Commodore 64	No differences
TRS-80	No differences

SECTION V
Control Statements

1. Which of the following is not an example of a control
    statement?
    a. IF/THEN   c. END
    b. GOTO   d. ON/GOTO

    *   *   *   *   *   *   *   *   *   *

    (c) The END statement is not a control statement.

2. Which of the following causes an unconditional transfer of
    control?
    a. IF/THEN   c. END
    b. GOTO   d. ON/GOTO

    *   *   *   *   *   *   *   *   *   *

    (b) The GOTO statement will transfer control to the
    transfer line number every time the statement is executed.

3. Which of the following is not true of the ON/GOTO state-
    ment?
    a. The value of the expression is always evaluated to an
        integer.
    b. The ON/GOTO statement is often used with menus.
    c. Since transfers depend upon the value of the expression
        the ON/GOTO is a conditional transfer statement.
    d. If the value of the ON/GOTO expression evaluates to 5,
        control is transferred to line 5.

    *   *   *   *   *   *   *   *   *   *

(d) If the value of the expression evaluates to 5, control is transferred to the fifth line number indicated in the ON/GOTO statement.

4.   Which of the following is not used to prevent an infinite loop?
a.   counters   c.   FOR/NEXT statements
b.   trailer values   d.   ON/GOTO statements

*   *   *   *   *   *   *   *   *   *

(d) The ON/GOTO statement is not used to control the number of times a loop is executed.

5.   Which of the following is not true when using counters?
a.   The counter value should not be changed when the loop is executed.
b.   The counter must be initialized before entering the loop.
c.   The counter must be incremented each time through the loop.
d.   The counter must be tested using the IF/THEN statement.

*   *   *   *   *   *   *   *   *   *

(a) The counter must be changed when the loop is executed. If is isn't, an infinite loop may result.

WORKSHEET

1.   Correct the following IF/THEN statements if necessary.
a.   10 IF N$ = LAST THEN 999   c.   100 IF X = J THEN 10
b.   20 IF X > 2 THEN   d.   210 IF N THEN 250

2.   Change the following program to produce the output listed.
```
10   PRINT "SWIMMER;# OF LAPS;
20   READ S$ ,L
30   IF S$ = END THEN 100
40   LET T = T + L
50   PRINT S$;L
60   GOTO 10
70   PRINT "TOTAL NUMBER OF LAPS SWUM WAS;L
80   DATA "DOL FIN",72,"SWORD FISH",10
90   DATA "CHARLIE TUNA",49
99   END
```

OUTPUT

```
SWIMMER          # OF LAPS
DOL FIN            72
SWORD FISH         10
CHARLIE TUNA       49

TOTAL NUMBER OF LAPS SWUM WAS 131
```

3. Rewrite the program in Question 2 using a counter for loop
    control.

4. What is wrong with the following program? Make the
    necessary correction(s).
    ```
    10 LET Z = 0
    20 PRINT Z;
    30 LET Z = Z + 3
    40 IF Z < 15 THEN 10
    50 END
    ```

5. What flowcharting symbol is used for the IF/THEN statement
    and the ON/GOTO statement?

6. What is looping? Why are loops useful?

7. Given the following flowchart, write the program.
    USE THIS DATA: SUGAR RAY, 133
                     MOHAMMED ALI, 144
                     LARRY HOLMES, 155
                     BEAT IT, 122
                     LAST, 0

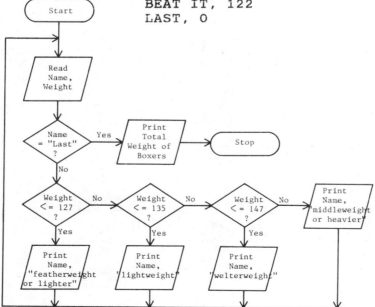

8.   When statement 40 is executed, control will be transferred
      to which statement?
         10 READ A,B
         20 LET A = A + B
         30 READ C
         40 ON C/A GOTO 99, 10, 30, 50
         50 DATA 10, 20, 30 10, 20, 60
         99 END

9.   What is a menu?

10.   What is a trailer value? How is it used? What kind of
      values should the programmer select for trailer values?

PROGRAMMING PROBLEM 1

The United States Government wants you to write a program to prepare a report listing all males who are 17 years old in order to send them information about draft registration. The program should use READ/DATA statements and should be able to run as many times as needed. The input data consists of the person's name, sex (M for Male and F for Female), and age. If the male's age is 17, he should be sent a letter. The report should be formatted as follows:

                    DRAFT INFORMATION REPORT

                              NAME
                    XXXXXXXXXXXXXXXXXX
                    XXXXXXXXXXXXXXXXXX
                    XXXXXXXXXXXXXXXXXX

The input data is given as follows:

NAME	SEX	AGE
John Hernadez	M	17
Laurie Ketchum	F	15
Paul Solomon	M	16
Frank Bradshaw	M	17
Tanya Young	F	17
Oswald Franklin	M	18
Thomas Conrad	M	17

PROGRAMMING PROBLEM 1 cont.

PROGRAMMING PROBLEM 2

Happy Hamburger fast food restaurant has a drive-through window open late at night. The manager of the restaurant needs a computer-driven menu to aid when the restaurant is busy. The customer reads the menu and then punches in what he wants to order. The computer then prints out the customer's bill including a 4 percent tax. The restaurant serves the following fast foods:

Hamburger	$ .80
Cheeseburger	$1.00
French Fries	$ .40
Cola	$ .50
Cookies	$ .60

Write a program with a menu using ON/GOTO statements that will total the customer's bill. Make sure the customer can order as many items as he wishes.

PROGRAMMING PROBLEM 2 cont.

ANSWER KEY

Worksheet

1.   a.   10 IF N$ = "LAST" THEN 999
      c.   20 IF X > 2 THEN 90
      d.   210 IF N = 3 THEN 250

3.   5   LET T = 0
      7   LET C = 0
      10   PRINT
      15   PRINT "SWIMMER","# OF LAPS"
      20   PRINT
      30   READ S$,L
      40   LET T = T + L
      45   LET C = C + 1
      50   PRINT S$,L
      60   IF C < 3 THEN 25
      65   PRINT
      70   PRINT "TOTAL NUMBER OF LAPS SWUM WAS",T
      80   DATA "DOL FIN",72,"SWORD FISH",10
      90   DATA "CHARLIE TUNA",49
      99   END

      RUNNH

      SWIMMER   # OF LAPS

      DOL FIN   72
      SWORD FISH   10
      CHARLIE TUNA   49

5.   The decision block: ⬦

7.
```
5     PRINT
10    LET T = 0
20    READ N$,W
30    IF N$ = "LAST" THEN 155
40    LET T = T + W
50    IF W < 127 THEN 100
60    IF W < 135 THEN 120
70    IF W < 147 THEN 140
80    PRINT N$,"MIDDLEWEIGHT OR HEAVIER"
90    GOTO 20
100   PRINT N$,"FEATHERWEIGHT OR LIGHTER"
110   GOTO 20
120   PRINT N$,"LIGHTWEIGHT"
130   GOTO 20
140   PRINT N$,"WELTERWEIGHT"
150   GOTO 20
155   PRINT
160   PRINT "THE TOTAL WEIGHT OF THE BOXERS IS";T
170   DATA "SUGAR RAY",133,"MOHAMMED ALI",144,"LARRY HOLMES",155
180   DATA "BEAT IT",122,"LAST",0
999   END

RUNNH

SUGAR RAY           LIGHTWEIGHT
MOHAMMED ALI        WELTERWEIGHT
LARRY HOLMES        MIDDLEWEIGHT OR HEAVIER
BEAT IT             FEATHERWEIGHT OR LIGHTER

THE TOTAL WEIGHT OF THE BOXERS IS 554
```

9. A menu is a listing that displays the functions that can be performed by a program. The desired function is chosen by the user when he or she enters a code (typically a simple numeric or alphabetic character).

PROGRAMMING PROBLEM 1

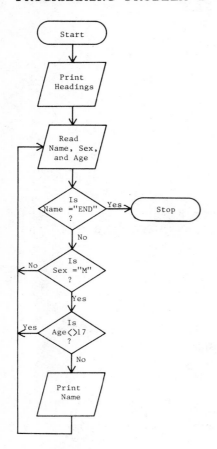

```
00100 REM ********************************************
00110 REM *** DRAFT INFORMATION REPORT PROGRAM ***
00120 REM ********************************************
00130 REM *** VARIABLES:                         ***
00140 REM ***   N$ = THE PERSON'S NAME           ***
00150 REM ***   S$ = THE PERSON'S SEX            ***
00160 REM ***   A = THE PERSON'S AGE             ***
00170 REM ********************************************
00180 REM ***           PRINT THE HEADINGS       ***
00190 REM ********************************************
00200 PRINT "DRAFT INFORMATION REPORT"
00210 PRINT
00220 PRINT TAB(5);"NAME"
00230 PRINT
00240 REM ********************************************
00250 REM *** IF PERSON'S SEX IS MALE AND HIS    ***
00260 REM *** AGE IS EQUAL TO SEVENTEEN, THEN    ***
00270 REM ***           PRINT HIS NAME           ***
00280 REM ********************************************
00290 READ N$,S$,A
00300 IF N$ = "END" THEN 999
00310 IF S$ = "M" THEN 330
00320 GOTO 290
00330 IF A <> 17 THEN 290
00340 PRINT N$
00350 GOTO 290
00360 REM ********************************************
00370 REM ***       THE DATA STATEMENTS          ***
00380 REM ********************************************
00390 DATA JOHN HERNADEZ,M,17
00400 DATA LAURIE KETCHUM,F,15
00410 DATA PAUL SOLOMON,M,16
00420 DATA FRANK BRADSHAW,M,17
00430 DATA TANYA YOUNG,F,17
00440 DATA OSWALD FRANKLIN,M,18
00450 DATA THOMAS CONRAD,M,17
00460 DATA END,END,0
00999 END


RUNNH
DRAFT INFORMATION REPORT

     NAME

JOHN HERNADEZ
FRANK BRADSHAW
THOMAS CONRAD
```

PSEUDOCODE

```
Start
Print the report headings
Start loop, do until name equals "END"
     Read name, sex, and age
     If sex = "M"
        Then
          If age = 17
             Then
                Print the name
          Endif
     Endif
End loop
Stop
```

MICROCOMPUTERS	
Apple	No differences
Apple Macintosh	No differences
IBM/Microsoft	No differences
PET Commodore 64	No differences
TRS-80	No differences

SECTION VI
More About Looping

STRUCTURED LEARNING

1. The FOR and NEXT statements are used primarily for
   a. unconditional transfers   c. printing data
   b. reading data   d. loop control

   *   *   *   *   *   *   *   *   *   *

   (d) The FOR and NEXT statements are used for concise loop
   control

2. Which of the following is not true of the FOR statement?
   a. It indicates the step value.
   b. It indicates the initial value.
   c. It adds the step value to the loop variable and then
      tests the loop control variable to see if it exceeds
      the terminal value.
   d. It indicates the terminal value.

   *   *   *   *   *   *   *   *   *   *

   (c) The NEXT statement increments the loop control variable
   and tests it against the terminal value.

3. In the following FOR statement 5 is the
        40 FOR I = 1 to 5 step 2
   a. initial value   c. loop variable
   b. terminal value   d. step value

   *   *   *   *   *   *   *   *   *   *

(b) 5 is the terminal value. When I (the loop variable) is greater than 5 the loop will terminate.

4.   Which of the following is not true of the STEP value?
      a.   When the step value is negative, the initial value must be equal to the terminal value.
      b.   The step value cannot be negative.
      c.   If the step value is positive, the initial value should be less than the terminal value.
      d.   If a step value is not indicated it is assumed to be one.

      *   *   *   *   *   *   *   *   *   *

(a) When the step value is negative, the initial value should be less than the terminal value.

5.   By how much will the index in the following FOR statement be incremented?
          100 FOR J = 10 TO 20 STEP 2
      a.   10   c.   2
      b.   20   d.   100

      *   *   *   *   *   *   *   *   *   *

(c) 2 is the step value that indicates how much the loop variable should be incremented. 100 is the line#, 10 is the initial value, and 20 is the terminal value.

WORKSHEET

1.   Give the value of each of the following where X = 2 and Y = 3.
          110 FOR K = (Y * 8) TO (2 ∧ Y) STEP -X
      a.   initial value =
      b.   terminal value =
      c.   step value
      d.   loop variable (2nd time thru loop) =

2.   Using FOR/NEXT statements, write a program to print the multiples of 5 from 100 down through 75.

3. What will be the output from the following program
    segments?
        (X = 9; Y = 4)
    a. 10   FOR I = (X - 8) TO 18 STEP Y
        20   PRINT I,
        30   NEXT I
        99   END

    b. 100   FOR Z = X TO -Y STEP -3
        110   PRINT Z; Z + 1
        120   NEXT Z
        999   END

    c. 50   FOR J = X TO X - 1
        60   PRINT J
        70   NEXT J
        99   END

4. Write a program using FOR/NEXT statements which will
    request a positive integer N, and prints N and N!
    (N! = N * (N - 1) * (N - 2) * (N - 3) . . . * (N - N + 1))

5. Write a program using FOR/NEXT statements which will read,
    print, and find the sum of the following numbers and print
    that result.
        99, -5, 201, 9, 27, 13, -7

6. Correct the following FOR/NEXT loops.
    a. 10 FOR I = 10 TO 1
            .
            .
            .
        50

    b. 20   FOR J = 2 TO 12 STEP 2
        30   LET S = S + J
        40   GOTO 20
        50   NEXT J

    c. 50   FOR K = 1 TO 10 STEP 2
        60   LET K = K + 1
        70   PRINT K
        80   NEXT K

```
d.  10   FOR X = 1 TO 10 STEP 1
    20     PRINT X
    30   LET S = X + 2
    40   NEXT I
```

7. Which of the following will print the average price of six books?

```
a.  10   LET S = 0              b.  10 FOR I = 1 TO 6
    20   FOR I = 1 TO 6             20    LET S = 0
    30     READ P                   30     READ P
    40     LET S = S + P            40     LET S = S + P
    50   NEXT I                     50 NEXT I
    60   LET A = S / 6              60 PRINT S / 6
    70   PRINT A                    70 DATA 5.95,3.23,4.97
    80   DATA 5.95, 3.23, 4.97      80 DATA 10.29,20.30,32. 97
    90   DATA 10.29,20.30,32.97     99 END
    99   END
```

8. Correct the following program segments.

```
a.  10   FOR I = 1 TO 10         b.  10 FOR I = 10 TO 5
    20     FOR J = 2 TO 4            20    FOR J = 3 TO 1
    30       IF (I + J) = 6 THEN 20  30       FOR K = 9 TO 12
    40       PRINT I,J                        .
    50     NEXT I                             .
    60   NEXT J                               .
                                    80        NEXT I
                                       NEXT J
                                   100 NEXT K
```

9. How many times will the statement PRINT I,J be executed in each of the following program segments?

```
a.  10   FOR I = 15 TO 3 STEP -3
    20     FOR J = 1 TO 3
    30       PRINT I,J
    40     NEXT J
    50   NEXT I

b.  10   FOR I = -8 TO 0 STEP 4
    20     FOR J = 1 TO 5 STEP 2
    30       FOR K = -2 TO 5 STEP 2
    40         PRINT I,J
    50       NEXT K
    60     NEXT J
    70   NEXT I
```

10.   What will be the output from the following program?
```
10   FOR N = 1 TO 2
20     FOR I = 1 TO 3
30       FOR J = 8 TO 10 STEP 2
40         PRINT N;I;J,
50       NEXT J
60       PRINT
70     NEXT I
80   NEXT N
99   END
```

PROGRAMMING PROBLEM 1

Your father wants to buy a new car with high gas mileage. He hates to look at numbers so he has asked you to write a program to print a bar chart of the gas mileage of a few economical cars that he has chosen. The bar chart is to contain the city mileage, highway mileage, and average (between city and highway) mileage. You can format the bar chart any way you wish but make sure that it contains a key for the different gas mileages and number line so that your father can determine the approximate gas mileage if he wishes.

The input data is as follows:

CAR	CITY MILEAGE	HIGHWAY MILEAGE
Chevrolet Chevette	19	34
Datsun 200SX	23	38
Dodge Omni	26	43
Ford Escort	21	42
Honda Civic	26	45

PROGRAMMING PROBLEM 1 cont.

PROGRAMMING PROBLEM 2

The University Honors Association is tutoring students for Math 124 and 125. The Association has asked you to write a program to print a report of the tutor and the student to be tutored. Write a program using FOR/NEXT loops to accomplish this task. The final report should look as follows:

TUTOR LIST

Tutor	Student
XXXXXXXXXXXXX	XXXXXXXXXXXXX
XXXXXXXXXXXXX	XXXXXXXXXXXXX
XXXXXXXXXXXXX	XXXXXXXXXXXXX
XXXXXXXXXXXXX	XXXXXXXXXXXXX

The data should be input using prompts and the INPUT statement. Use the following data to test your program:

TUTOR	STUDENT
Kathi Johnson	Lonnie MacArthur
Pat Willis	Barry Moore
Alan Rath	Karen Holland
Jennifer Loring	Martha Edison
Donna Cornell	Randy Parsons

PROGRAMMING PROBLEM 2 cont.

ANSWER KEY

Worksheet

1. a. 24
    b. 8
    c. -2
    d. 22

3. a.
    1   5   9   13   17

    b.
        9   10
        6   7
        3   4
        0   1
       -3   -2

    c. Nothing will be output because the loop is not exe-
        cuted. The initial values exceeds the terminal value
        before the loop is ever executed.

5.   10   LET S = 0
        20   FOR I = 1 TO 7
        30   READ N
        40   PRINT N;
        50   LET S = S + N
        60   NEXT I
        70   PRINT
        80   PRINT "THE SUM IS ";S
        90   DATA 99,-5,201,9,27,13,-7
        99   END

7. a

9. a. 15
    b. 36

PROGRAMMING PROBLEM 1

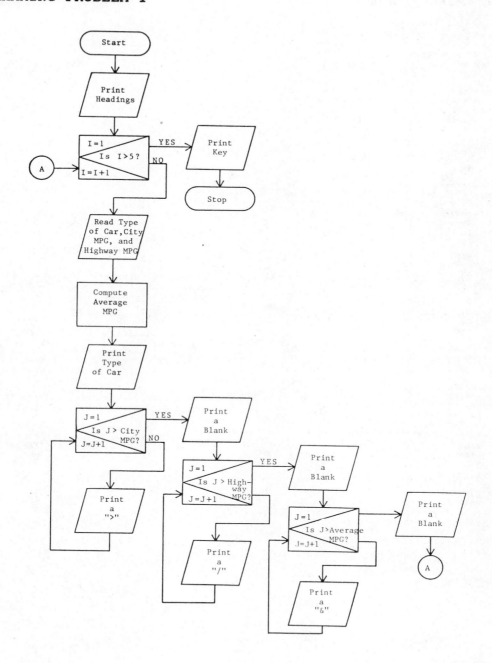

PROGRAMMING PROBLEM 1 con't.

```
00010 REM ****************************
00020 REM *** GAS MILEAGE PROGRAM ***
00030 REM ****************************
00040 REM *** VARIABLES:          ***
00050 REM ***   C$ = TYPE OF CAR  ***
00060 REM ***   C = CITY MPG      ***
00070 REM ***   H = HIGHWAY MPG   ***
00080 REM ***   A = AVERAGE MPG   ***
00090 REM ****************************
00100 REM *** PRINT THE HEADINGS  ***
00110 REM ****************************
00120 PRINT
00130 PRINT
00140 PRINT
00150 PRINT "GAS MILEAGE CHART"
00160 PRINT
00170 PRINT TAB(14);"        10       20      30      40"
00180 REM ****************************
00190 REM *** COMPUTE AVERAGE AND ***
00200 REM *** PRINT THE BAR CHART ***
00210 REM ****************************
00220 FOR I = 1 TO 5
00230    READ C$,C,H
00240    LET A = (C + H) / 2
00250    PRINT C$
00260    PRINT TAB(14);
00270    FOR J = 1 TO C
00280       PRINT ">";
00290    NEXT J
00300    PRINT
00310    PRINT TAB(14);
00320    FOR J = 1 TO H
00330       PRINT "/";
00340    NEXT J
00350    PRINT
00360    PRINT TAB(14);
00370    FOR J = 1 TO A
00380       PRINT "&";
00390    NEXT J
00400    PRINT
00410 NEXT I
00420 REM ****************************
00430 REM *** PRINT KEY TO CHART  ***
00440 REM ****************************
00450 PRINT
00460 PRINT
00470 PRINT "KEY:"
00480 PRINT
00490 PRINT "> = CITY MPG"
00500 PRINT "/ = HIGHWAY MPG"
00510 PRINT "& = AVERAGE MPG"
00520 REM ****************************
00530 REM *** THE DATA STATEMENTS ***
00540 REM ****************************
00550 DATA CHEVROLET CHEVETTE,19,34
00560 DATA DATSUN 200SX,23,38
00570 DATA DODGE OMNI,26,43
00580 DATA FORD ESCORT,21,42
00590 DATA HONDA CIVIC,26,45
00999 END
```

```
RUNNH

GAS MILEAGE CHART

                  10       20      30      40
CHEVROLET CHEVETTE
             >>>>>>>>>>>>>>>>>>>
             ///////////////////////////////////
             &&&&&&&&&&&&&&&&&&&&&&&&&&&
DATSUN 200SX
             >>>>>>>>>>>>>>>>>>>>>>>
             //////////////////////////////////////
             &&&&&&&&&&&&&&&&&&&&&&&&&&&&&&&
DODGE OMNI
             >>>>>>>>>>>>>>>>>>>>>>>>>>
             //////////////////////////////////////////
             &&&&&&&&&&&&&&&&&&&&&&&&&&&&&&&&&&&
FORD ESCORT
             >>>>>>>>>>>>>>>>>>>>>
             ///////////////////////////////////////////
             &&&&&&&&&&&&&&&&&&&&&&&&&&&&&&&
HONDA CIVIC
             >>>>>>>>>>>>>>>>>>>>>>>>>>
             //////////////////////////////////////////
             &&&&&&&&&&&&&&&&&&&&&&&&&&&&&&&&&&&

KEY:

> = CITY MPG
/ = HIGHWAY MPG
& = AVERAGE MPG
```

MICROCOMPUTERS

Apple	Output must be reformatted
Apple Macintosh	No differences
IBM/Microsoft	No differences
PET Commodore 64	No differences
TRS-80	No differences

PSEUDOCODE

```
Start
Print the report headings
Start loop, do five times
    Read type of car, city MPG, and highway MPG
    Average equals (city MPG + highway MPG) / 2
    Print type of car
    Print spaces to column 14
    Start loop, do city MPG times
      print ">"
End loop
Print a blank
Print spaces to column 14
Start loop, do average MPG times
    Print "&"
End loop
Print bar chart key
End
```

SECTION VII
Functions

1. Which of the following statements assigns 3 to R?
    a. 10 LET R = SGN(3)   c. 30 LET R = INT(-3)
    b. 10 LET R = INT(2.8)   d. 50 LET R = ABS(-3)

    *   *   *   *   *   *   *   *   *   *

    (d) Answer a. assigns 1 to R, b. assigns 2 to R and c.
    assigns -3 to R. The statement in d. assigns the absolute
    value of -3 which is 3, to R.

2. The INT function
    a. computes the lowest integer greater than or equal to
        its argument
    b. computes the greatest integer less than or equal to its
        argument
    c. rounds numbers to the nearest integer
    d. cannot be used with negative numbers

    *   *   *   *   *   *   *   *   *   *

    (b) The INT function computes the greatest integer less
    than or equal to its argument.

3.   The general format of the statement used by the programmer
      to define his or her own function is
      a.   line#   DEFINE   function name(argument) = expression
      b.   line#   DEF   function name(argument) = expression
      c.   line#   USERDEF   function name(argument) = expression
      d.   line#   FUNCTION   function name(argument) = expression

      *   *   *   *   *   *   *   *   *   *

      (b) The statement used to define a function is DEF. Its
      general format is: line# DEF function name(argument) =
      expression.

4.   Which of the following is not a trigonometric function?
      a.   CO(X)   c.   ATN(X)
      b.   SIN(X)   d.   TAN(X)

      *   *   *   *   *   *   *   *   *   *

      (a) The fourth trigonometric function defined in the BASIC
      language is COS(X).

5.   Which of the following is not an exponential function?
      a.   LOG(X)   c.   RND(X)
      b.   EXP(X)   d.   SQR(X)

      *   *   *   *   *   *   *   *   *   *

      (c) The RND function is used to generate random numbers.

WORKSHEET

1.   Using the following values for X, what value will be
      returned by SGN(X)?
      a.   0   c.   -7.32
      b.   -1   d.   8.9

2.   Using the following values for X, what value will be
      returned by INT(X)?
      a.   99.9   c.   -4.7
      b.   99.2   d.   -5.2

3.   Write a statement using a library function that branches if
      a checking account is overdrawn. The balance of the
      checking account is contained in B.

4.   Write the instruction(s), using the INT function, that will
      round X to the nearest hundredth.

5.   What does the RND function do?   (be specific)

6.   What is a library function?   Give four examples.

7.   What are the values of A and B after the following program
      has been executed?
      ```
      10   LET A = 9
      20   LET B = SQR(A)
      30   LET A = INT(B * 1.5)
      99   END
      ```

8.   Correct the following invalid statements.
      ```
      a.   10   LET X = 5 * TAN
      b.   20   PRINT SR(16)
      c.   30   IF ABS(X) < O THEN 60
      d.   40   DEFINE FN(X) = X + 3 * X∧2
      ```

9.   What is wrong with the following program?
      ```
      30   LET Z = 17
      40   LET X = FNR(Z)
      50   PRINT Z,X
      60   DEF FNR(T) = (T + 90) * 2
      ```

10.   Write a function definition to generate a random number
      between 1 and 10.

PROGRAMMING PROBLEM 1

The Eddies Canning Company is planning to bottle fruit juice in an aluminum can. The company wants you to write a program to calculate the volume of each can. The company also needs the volume to be rounded to the nearest integer so they can determine which can is the best choice for bottling fruit juice. The formula for volume of a cylinder is given below:

$$2(3.1416) \ (RADIUS \wedge 2) \ (HEIGHT)$$

The types of cylinders that the company is considering are listed below:

Radius	Height
3	4
5	6
7	8

PROGRAMMING PROBLEM 1 cont.

PROGRAMMING PROBLEM 2

Your Math 300 teacher has assigned some homework problems to you. You need to find the Cosine, Sine, and Tangent of some angles in radians. You have already completed your homework but would like to write a computer program to find the answers so you can see if you have the right answers. Following are the angles in radians your teacher gave to you (note there are twenty angles):

```
63.5
34.9
78
90.5
50
45
-89
-54
-72
-65
-12
128
175
289
301
345
215
222
109
199
```

PROGRAMMING PROBLEM 2 cont.

ANSWER KEY

Worksheet

1.   a. 0
      b. −1
      c. −1
      d. 1

3.   100 IF SGN(B) = −1 THEN 200

5.   The RND function generates a random number between 0 and 1.

7.   A = 4
      B = 3

9.   The function FNR(T) must be defined before the function
      call in line 40.

PROGRAMMING PROBLEM 1

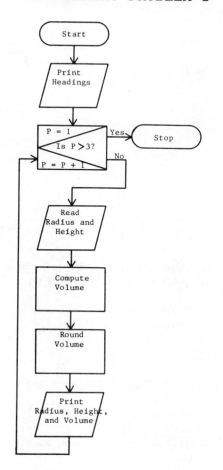

```
00100 REM ****************************************
00110 REM *** VOLUME OF A CYLINDER PROGRAM ***
00120 REM ****************************************
00130 REM *** VARIABLES:                       ***
00140 REM ***    R = RADIUS OF THE CAN         ***
00150 REM ***    H = HEIGHT OF THE CAN         ***
00160 REM ***    V = VOLUME OF THE CAN         ***
00170 REM ****************************************
00180 REM ***   PRINT THE REPORT HEADINGS     ***
00190 REM ****************************************
00200 PRINT "VOLUME REPORT"
00210 PRINT
00220 PRINT "RADIUS","HEIGHT","VOLUME"
00230 PRINT
00240 REM ****************************************
00250 REM ***   COMPUTE VOLUME OF THE CAN     ***
00260 REM ****************************************
00270 FOR P = 1 TO 3
00280    READ R,H
00290    LET V = (2 * 3.1416) * (R ^ 2 * H)
00300    LET V = INT((V * 10 + 0.5) / 10)
00310    PRINT R,H,V
00320 NEXT P
00330 REM ****************************************
00340 REM ***       THE DATA STATEMENTS       ***
00350 REM ****************************************
00360 DATA 3,4,5,6,7,8
00999 END

RUNNH
VOLUME REPORT
```

RADIUS	HEIGHT	VOLUME
3	4	226
5	6	942
7	8	2463

PSEUDOCODE

```
Start
Print the report headings
Start loop, do three times
  Read radius and height
  Compute volume
  Round the volume
  Print radius, height, and volume
End loop
Stop
```

MICROCOMPUTERS	
Apple	No differences
Apple Macintosh	No differences
IBM/Microsoft	No differences
PET Commodore 64	No differences
TRS-80	No differences

SECTION VIII
Subroutines and String Functions

STRUCTURED LEARNING

1. A sequence of instructions outside of the main body of the program that may be executed as many times as necessary, but typed only once is called a
    a. module   c. routine
    b. procedure   d. subroutine

    *   *   *   *   *   *   *   *   *   *

    (d) A subroutine needs to be typed only once, but may be executed as often as necessary.

2. The GOSUB statement
    a. is used to transfer the flow of control from the main body of the program to a subroutine
    b. is a conditional transfer statement
    c. is used to transfer the flow of control from a subroutine to the main body of the program
    d. may appear only once in a program

    *   *   *   *   *   *   *   *   *   *

    (a) The GOSUB statement unconditionally transfers the flow of control from the main body of the program to a subroutine.

3.   The RETURN statement
      a.   is used to transfer the flow of control from the main
            body of the program to a subroutine
      b.   is a conditional transfer statement
      c.   is used to transfer the flow of control from a
            subroutine to the main body of the program
      d.   helps the computer remember where to return after the
            subroutine has been executed

      *   *   *   *   *   *   *   *   *   *

      (c) Unconditionally transfers the flow of control from a
      subroutine to the main body of the program.

4.   The STOP statement
      a.   may only appear once in a program
      b.   must be the highest numbered statement in a program
      c.   is used instead of an END statement
      d.   halts execution of a program

      *   *   *   *   *   *   *   *   *   *

      (d) The STOP statement halts the execution of a program.
      There may be several STOP statements within a program.

5.   Instructions that help the computer to prevent "garbage in-
      garbage out" errors are called
      a.   garbage locators
      b.   error subroutines
      c.   exception-handling instructions
      d.   GIGO instructions

      *   *   *   *   *   *   *   *   *   *

      (c) Exception handling instructions are sequences of state-
      ments which help the computer prevent the input of invalid
      data, which is referred to as a garbage in-garbage out
      error.

WORKSHEET

1.   Write a program statement that will concatenate the following two strings.

        A$ = "WORKIN AT THE CAR "
        B$ = "WASH BLUES"

2.   Write a program to accept a word and print out the number of characters in that word.

3.   Write a program to print the input word BACKWARDS.

4.   Write a program to output the following.

        D
        A
        Y
        T
        O
        N
        A

        B
        E
        A
        C
        H

5.   What will be printed by the following statement?

        10 PRINT RIGHT$("OFFSHORE",4)

6.   Which of the following will print the five left-most characters of the string stored in A$?

        a.   10 PRINT LEFT$(A$,5)
        b.   20 PRINT LEFT$(5,A$)
        c.   30 PRINT LEFT$(A$,1,5)
        d.   40 PRINT LEFT$(1,5,A$)

7.   What are two common uses of the STOP statement?

8.   What do the CHR$ and a ASCII functions do?

9.   What does the VAL function do? Why is it useful? What function does the opposite of the VAL function?

10.   Correct any invalid statements.

      a.   20 LET A$ = ASCII("HOME")
      b.   30 LET B$ = VAL("123.9")
      c.   40 LET X = CHR(62)
      d.   50 IF LEN(B$) < 10 THEN 100

PROGRAMMING PROBLEM 1

Your grandmother just gave you $200.00 for being nice to her. You have decided to buy clothes with the money. Since you only have $200.00 for clothes, you have decided to write a program to help you spend your money. The program uses an INPUT statement to enter the cost of each item of clothing that you buy. Then the program goes to a subroutine to compute and print the total you have spent thus far. If the total is under $200.00, the computer will ask you to enter another price. Thus the computer keeps going until you have reached your $200.00 limit. After you have reached the limit, the computer prints out a message for you.

Use the following prices to test your program:

```
85.55
15.45
99.00
```

PROGRAMMING PROBLEM 1 cont.

PROGRAMMING PROBLEM 2

The Richland Boys Institute for Higher Education has completed its enrollment for the fall term. The Admissions Officer has asked you to write a program that will print letters to those students who have been accepted to the school. The letter should be written as follows:

Dear Mr. XXXXX

Congratulations!

You have been admitted to our fine institution. Please contact our department by July 18 if you wish to attend. Once again, congratulations!

                        Sincerely yours,

                        Pauline Harris
                        Admissions Officer

The program should work for any number of students. The names of the students are to be entered with INPUT statements. Use the following names as test data:

Greg Allgair
Bill Haidle

The letter should be addressed to the student's last name. Therefore you must take the input data and compute the student's last name in the program. No cheating.

PROGRAMMING PROBLEM 2 cont.

ANSWER KEY

Worksheet

1.   20 LET C$ = A$ + B$

3.   10 INPUT "ENTER A WORD";W$
      20 FOR I = LEN(W$) to 1 STEP −1
      30   PRINT MID$(W$,I,1);
      40 NEXT I

5.   SHORE

7.   The STOP statement is placed before subroutines to indicate
      the logical end of the program and to keep the subroutine
      from being executed unnecessarily. It is also used in
      exception handling routines.

9.   The VAL function converts a numerical string to a numerical
      value. It's useful in that it allows a number in a
      character string to be converted so that it can be used in
      mathematical operations. The STR$ function works just the
      opposite of the VAL function.

PROGRAMMING PROBLEM 1

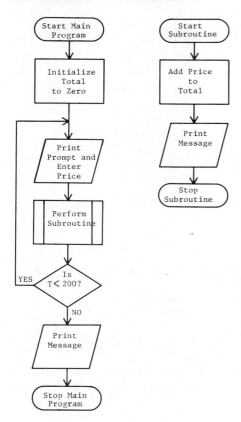

```
00100 REM *************************************
00110 REM *** FALL CLOTHING SPREE PROGRAM ***
00120 REM *************************************
00130 REM *** VARIABLES:                    ***
00140 REM ***    T = TOTAL AMOUNT SPENT      ***
00150 REM ***    C = EACH CLOTHING AMOUNT    ***
00160 REM *************************************
00170 REM *** INITIALIZE TOTAL/ENTER DATA ***
00180 REM *************************************
00190 LET T = 0
00200 PRINT "HOW MUCH DID IT COST?"
00210 INPUT C
00220 REM *************************************
00230 REM ***         COMPUTE TOTAL        ***
00240 REM *************************************
00250 GOSUB 500
00260 REM *************************************
00270 REM ***      IF TOTAL >= 200 THEN    ***
00280 REM ***        STOP ELSE CONTINUE    ***
00290 REM *************************************
00300 IF T < 200 THEN 200
00310 REM *************************************
00320 REM ***         ENDING MESSAGE       ***
00330 REM *************************************
00340 PRINT
00350 PRINT
00360 PRINT
00370 PRINT "I HOPE YOU HAD FUN"
00380 PRINT
00390 PRINT
00400 STOP
00500 REM *************************************
00510 REM *** SUBROUTINE TO COMPUTE TOTAL ***
00520 REM *************************************
00530 LET T = T + C
00540 PRINT
00550 PRINT "YOU HAVE SPENT $";T;" ON CLOTHES THUS FAR"
00560 PRINT
00570 RETURN
00999 END


RUNNH

HOW MUCH DID IT COST?
 ? 85.55

YOU HAVE SPENT $ 85.55   ON CLOTHES THUS FAR

HOW MUCH DID IT COST?
 ? 15.45

YOU HAVE SPENT $ 101   ON CLOTHES THUS FAR

HOW MUCH DID IT COST?
 ? 99

YOU HAVE SPENT $ 200   ON CLOTHES THUS FAR


I HOPE YOU HAD FUN

STOP at lIne 00400 of MAIN PROGRAM
```

PSEUDOCODE

```
Start main program
Initialize total to zero
Start loop, do until total >= 200
  Print prompt
  Enter price
  Perform total subroutine
End loop
Print message
Stop main program
Start total subroutine
Add price to total
Print message
Stop total subroutine
```

MICROCOMPUTERS	
Apple	No differences
Apple Macintosh	No differences
IBM/Microsoft	No differences
PET Commodore 64	No differences
TRS-80	No differences

SECTION IX
Arrays

STRUCTURED LEARNING

1. A(n) _____ is a group of storage locations in memory in which data elements can be stored.
    a. DIM
    b. subscript
    c. array
    d. section

    *   *   *   *   *   *   *   *   *   *

    (c) An array is a group of storage locations in memory in which data elements can be stored. The array is given one name.

2. Subscripts
    a. are used to indicate individual elements in an array
    b. can be negative
    c. may not be mathematical expressions
    d. are used to indicate the address in memory of a simple variable

    *   *   *   *   *   *   *   *   *   *

    (a) Subscripts are used to indicate individual elements in an array.

3. References to specific elements of arrays are called
    a. unsubscripted variables
    b. subscripted variables
    c. array variables
    d. element variables

    *   *   *   *   *   *   *   *   *   *

(b) Subscripted variables are references to specific elements of an array.

4.   An array with rows and columns is called
     a.   a one-dimensional array
     b.   a two-dimensional array
     c.   a three-dimensional array
     d.   a list

     *   *   *   *   *   *   *   *   *   *

     (b) A two-dimensional array is an array with rows and columns.

5.   If an array is to contain more than ten elements, the programmer can specify the number of elements the array will contain using a
     a.   DCL statement (short for declare)
     b.   DIM statement (short for dimension)
     c.   SPEC statement (short for specification)
     d.   RES statement (short for reserve)

     *   *   *   *   *   *   *   *   *   *

     (b) Compilers will automatically reserve space for ten elements in an array. If an array is to contain more than ten elements, the number of elements which space must be reserved for is specified in a DIM (short for dimension) statement.

WORKSHEET

1.   What will be the values of the following, given these arrays and simple variables.

ARRAY X	ARRAY Z	
50	1	I = 1
100	2	J = 3
25	30	K = 4
125	16	

     a.   X(K)   d.   Z(I + 3)
     b.   Z(K - J)   e.   Z(2) - Z(I)
     c.   X(I) + X(J)   f.   X(J - I)

2.   What will be the values in array A after the following
      program segment is executed?
```
10    FOR J = 10 TO 1 STEP -2
20       READ A(J)
30    NEXT J
40    DATA  10,2,9,5,12
50    DATA  20,22,98,73,7
```

3.   Write a BASIC statement that will reserve storage locations
      for an array named N that will contain 99 elements.

4.   What will be the output from the following program?
```
10    FOR I = 1 TO 6
20       READ X(I)
30    NEXT I
40    FOR J = 1 TO 6 STEP 3
50       PRINT X(J), X(J + 1), X(J + 2)
60    NEXT J
70    DATA 9, 8, 7, 6, 5, 4
99    END
```

5.   How many storage locations are reserved for the array R by
      the following statement?   15 DIM (20,5)

6.   Given the array and variables below what will be the value
      of the following?

	ARRAY T		
55	105	205	I = 1
475	155	395	J = 2
385	995	765	K = 4

a. T(I,J)   d. T(J,K - J)
b. T(J,I)   e. T(J,J)
c. T(K - I,I)   f. T(I,I + J)

7. What will be the output of the following program?
```
 5 DIM X(3,4)
10   FOR I = 1 TO 3
20     FOR J = 1 TO 4
30       READ X(I,J)
40       PRINT X(I,J),
50     NEXT J
60     PRINT
70   NEXT I
80   DATA  7, 9, 22, 1, 36, 5
90   DATA  11, 6, 12, 32 ,10, 49
99   END
```

8. Write a program that will read the values below into a two-
    dimensional array and print the total of the elements in
    the second column.

1	3	9
12	15	18
21	24	27
30	33	36

9. Write a program segment that will total the rows of the
    array G with the dimensions (3,5), and place those totals
    in another array R.

10. Write a program segment to total all the elements of array
    W with the dimensions (4,3).

PROGRAMMING PROBLEM 1

There are four grocery stores in town, Kathy's supermarket, Key Food, Church's, and The Market Place. The local consumer group has decided to do some testing of the prices of foods at the various stores. The consumer group has asked you to write a program to determine which store has the best bargains on hamburger, lettuce, and bread. Write a program that prints a report of the various prices at the stores and also prints the store which has the best food buys. The prices are listed below:

	Hamburger	Lettuce	Bread
Kathy's Supermarket	1.08/lb	0.99/head	0.35/loaf
Key Food	1.11/lb	0.89/head	0.40/loaf
Church's	0.99/lb	0.99/head	0.45/loaf
The Market Place	1.18/lb	0.89/head	0.38/loaf

PROGRAMMING PROBLEM 1 cont.

PROGRAMMING PROBLEM 2

The University newspaper is planning to print a comic section with their paper. The editor of the paper has asked you to print a list of the comic strips in alphabetical order. The comic strips to be printed are as follows:

Peanuts
Heathcliff
Herman
Dennis the Menace
Dick Tracy
Family Circus
Mary Worth
Li'l Abner
Superman
Beetle Bailey
Hagar the Horrible
The Wizard of ID
Brenda Starr
B.C.
Spiderman

PROGRAMMING PROBLEM 2 cont.

ANSWER KEY

Worksheet

1. a. 125   d. 16
    b. 1   e. 1
    c. 75   f. 100

3.   10 DIM N(99)

5.   100

7.   7   9   22   1
      36   5   11   6
      12   32   10   49

9.   10   LET R(1) = 0
      20   LET R(2) = 0
      30   LET R(3) = 0
      40   FOR I = 1 TO 3
      50   FOR J = 1 TO 5
      60   LET R(I) = R(I) + G(I,J)
      70   NEXT J
      80   NEXT I

PROGRAMMING PROBLEM 1

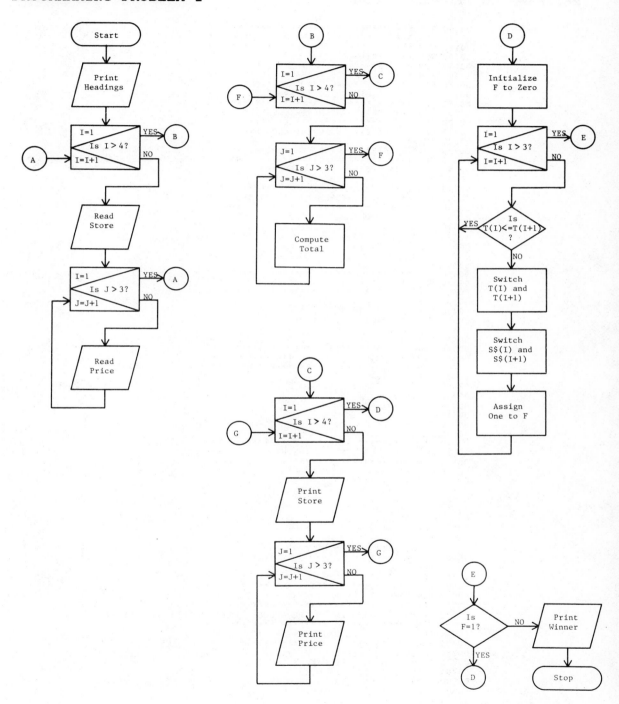

PROGRAMMING PROBLEM 1 cont.

```
00100 REM ***********************************
00110 REM *** GROCERY STORE PRICE PROGRAM ***
00120 REM ***********************************
00130 REM *** VARIABLES:                  ***
00140 REM ***   S$ = NAME OF THE STORE    ***
00150 REM ***    P = PRICE OF EACH ITEM   ***
00160 REM ***    T = TOTAL FOR EACH STORE ***
00170 REM ***  F,H,H$ = SORT VARIABLES    ***
00180 REM ***********************************
00190 REM ***   PRINT THE REPORT HEADINGS  ***
00200 REM ***********************************
00210 PRINT TAB(22);"THE GREAT GROCERY WAR"
00220 PRINT
00230 PRINT TAB(23);"PRICE PER";TAB(41);"PRICE PER";TAB(55);"PRICE PER"
00240 PRINT TAB(4);"STORE";TAB(21);"LB HAMBURGER";TAB(39);"HEAD/LETTUCE";
00250 PRINT TAB (53);"LOAF OF BREAD"
00260 PRINT
00270 REM ***********************************
00280 REM ***  READ STORE AND ITS PRICES  ***
00290 REM ***********************************
00300 FOR I = 1 TO 4
00310   READ S$(I)
00320   FOR J = 1 TO 3
00330     READ P(I,J)
00340   NEXT J
00350 NEXT I
00360 REM ***********************************
00370 REM ***      COMPUTE TOTAL PRICE     ***
00380 REM ***********************************
00390 FOR I = 1 TO 4
00400   FOR J = 1 TO 3
00410     LET T(I) = T(I) + P(I,J)
00420   NEXT J
00430 NEXT I
00440 REM ***********************************
00450 REM *** PRINT STORE AND ITS PRICES  ***
00460 REM ***********************************
00470 FOR I = 1 TO 4
00480   PRINT S$(I);TAB(24);
00490   FOR J = 1 TO 3
00500     PRINT P(I,J),
00510   NEXT J
00520 PRINT
00530 NEXT I
00540 REM ***********************************
00550 REM ***       COMPUTE THE WINNER     ***
00560 REM ***********************************
00570 LET F = 0
00580 FOR I = 1 TO 3
00590   IF T(I) <= T(I + 1) THEN 670
00600     LET H = T(I)
00610     LET H$ = S$(I)
00620     LET T(I) = T(I + 1)
00630     LET S$(I) = S$(I + 1)
00640     LET R(I + 1) = H
00650     LET S$(I + 1) = H$
00660     LET F = 1
00670 NEXT I
00680 IF F = 1 THEN 570
00690 REM ***********************************
00700 REM ***        PRINT THE WINNER      ***
00710 REM ***********************************
00720 PRINT "THE WINNER OF THE GROCERY WARS CONTEST IS ";S$(1)
00730 REM ***********************************
00740 REM ***      THE DATA STATEMENTS     ***
00750 REM ***********************************
00760 :'LLLLLLLLLLLLLLLLLL      ##.##       ##.##       ##.##
00770 DATA KATHY'S SUPERMARKET,1.08,0.99,0.35
00780 DATA KEY FOOD,1.11,0.89,0.40
00790 DATA CHURCH'S,0.99,0.99,0.38
00800 DATA THE MARKET PLACE,1.18,0.89,0.40
00999 END
```

PROGRAMMING PROBLEM 1 cont.

```
RUNNH
                    THE GREAT GROCERY WAR

                  PRICE PER       PRICE PER     PRICE PER
       STORE      LB HAMBURGER   HEAD/LETTUCE  LOAF OF BREAD

KATHY'S SUPERMARKET     1.08          0.99          0.35
KEY FOOD                1.11          0.89          0.4
CHURCH'S                0.99          0.99          0.38
THE MARKET PLACE        1.18          0.89          0.4
THE WINNER OF THE GROCERY WARS CONTEST IS CHURCH'S
```

PSEUDOCODE

```
Start
Print the report headings
Start loop, do four times
  Read name of store
  Start loop, do three times
    Read price of each item from each store
  End loop
End loop
Start loop, do four times
  Start loop, do three times
    Compute total for each store
  End loop
End loop
Start loop, do four times
  Print store name and tab to column 24
  Start loop, do three times
    Print price of each item from each store
  End loop
End loop
Sort the stores from lowest total price to highest total price
Print the store with the lowest total price
Stop
```

MICROCOMPUTERS	
Apple	Output must be reformatted
Apple Macintosh	No differences
IBM/Microsoft	No differences
PET Commodore 64	Output must be reformatted
TRS-80	Output must be reformatted

SECTION X
File Processing

1. Which of the following is true of files?
    a. Data statements are always necessary when using files.
    b. They usually store data on secondary storage devices.
    c. There is only one type of file access method--
        sequential access.
    d. There is a standardized method for performing opera-
        tions on files.

    *   *   *   *   *   *   *   *   *

    (b) Files store data on secondary storage devices elimi-
    nating the need for DATA statements. There are two methods
    of file access: sequential and random. Unfortunately,
    there is no standard method for file processing.

2. Sequential files usually contain data items that
    a. are likely to change frequently
    b. are ordered one right after the other in the same order
        they are entered
    c. are numerical values
    d. may be read from the file in any order

    *   *   *   *   *   *   *   *   *

    (b) The data items in sequential files are ordered one
    right after another in the same order they were entered.

80

3.   A group of one or more related fields is known as
      a.   an individual data item   c.   a file
      b.   grouped fields   d.   a record

      *   *   *   *   *   *   *   *   *

      (d) A record is a group of one or more related fields.

4.   A group of one or more related records is known as
      a.   a file   c.   a field
      b.   grouped records   d.   a data item

      *   *   *   *   *   *   *   *   *

      (a) A group of one or more related records is a file.

5.   A typical sequence of steps when working with files is
      a.   open, write, close   c.   close, write, open
      b.   open, close, write   d.   close, open, write

      *   *   *   *   *   *   *   *   *

      (a) Sequential files must be opened to be written to and
      then closed after data has been written to them.

WORKSHEET

1.   Write the statements necessary to open for output and then
      close the file named BOOKS.

2.   Give the statement which will write the contents of the
      variables N$,S to file number 2.

3.   Why must a file be closed after it has been accessed?

4.   What are fields, files, and records?

5.   Given a file that contains ten item names with
      corresponding quantities and unit prices, write the state-
      ments which will input the entire file into three arrays,
      N$, Q, and P.

6.   Write a program which creates a file, called GROCERIES, and stores ten items in it.

7.   What are random files?

PROGRAMMING PROBLEM 1

Your uncle is starting a book collection and he has asked you to write a program to store his book titles and their authors in a data disk file. First sort the list by book titles (remember to take the authors along with the titles) and then create a file for the books. Use the following books as the data for your file.

BOOK TITLE	AUTHOR
Think and Grow Rich	Napoleon Hill
Computers and Data Processing	Steve Mandell
Economics	Paul Samuelson
Information Processing	Marilyn Bohl
The Snows of Kilimanjaro	Ernest Hemingway
Cost and Managerial Accounting	Ronald Hartley

PROGRAMMING PROBLEM 1 cont.

PROGRAMMING PROBLEM 2

Your uncle has recently bought more books. He would like to update the book file created in Programming Problem 1. Update the book file (making sure that all of the books are in alphabetic order by the book title) and then print the contents of the file in a report format. Use the following books and their authors to update the file.

BOOK TITLE	AUTHOR
Gone With the Wind	Margaret Mitchell
Understanding Computers	Steve Mandell
A Christmas Carol	Charles Dickens
Hamlet	William Shakespeare
In Search of Excellence	Thomas Peters

PROGRAMMING PROBLEM 2 cont.

ANSWER KEY

Worksheet

1.   10   OPEN "BOOKS" AS FILE #3
         .
         .
         .
     50   CLOSE #3

3.   A file must be closed after accessing to prevent loss of its contents and also to indicate to the computer that the use of the file is finished for the present time.

5.   10   OPEN "LIST" AS FILE #2
     20   FOR I = 1 TO   10
     30   INPUT #2,N$(I),Q(I),P(I)
     40   NEXT I
     50   CLOSE #2
     99   END

7.   Random data files are files that allow you to read or write from file in random order. So you may access a record without reading all previous records.

PROGRAMMING PROBLEM 1

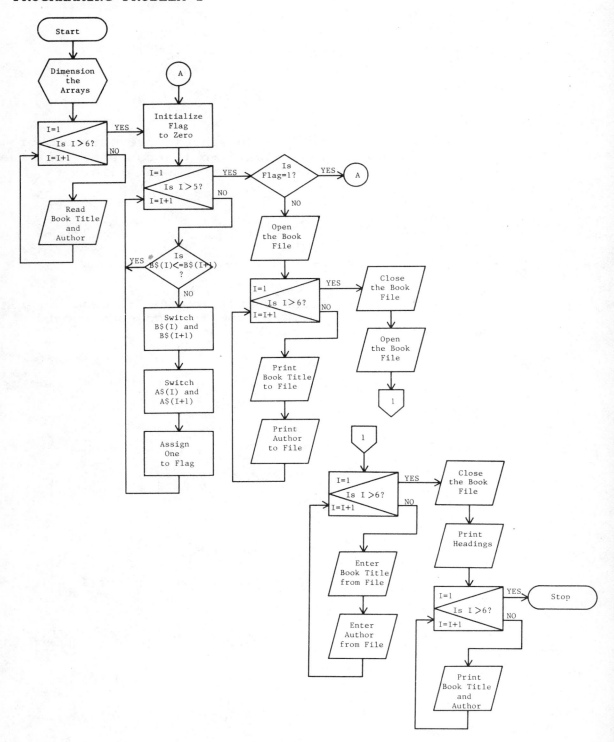

PROGRAMMING PROBLEM 1 cont.

```
00010 REM **********************************
00020 REM *** BOOK COLLECTION FILE PROGRAM ***
00030 REM **********************************
00040 REM *** VARIABLES:                 ***
00050 REM ***    B$ = NAME OF THE BOOK    ***
00060 REM ***    A$ = AUTHOR OF THE BOOK  ***
00070 REM **********************************
00080 REM ***  DIM ARRAYS AND READ DATA   ***
00090 REM **********************************
00100 DIM B$(20),A$(20)
00110 FOR I = 1 TO 6
00120   READ B$(I),A$(I)
00130 NEXT I
00140 REM **********************************
00150 REM *** SORT THE BOOKS BY BOOK TITLE ***
00160 REM **********************************
00170 LET F = 0
00180 FOR I = 1 TO 5
00190   IF B$(I) <= B$(I + 1) THEN 270
00200   LET H1$ = B$(I)
00210   LET H2$ = A$(I)
00220   LET B$(I) = B$(I + 1)
00230   LET A$(I) = A$(I + 1)
00240   LET B$(I + 1) = H1$
00250   LET A$(I + 1) = H2$
00260   LET F = 1
00270 NEXT I
00280 IF F = 1 THEN 170
00290 REM **********************************
00300 REM *** WRITE TITLE & AUTHOR TO FILE  ***
00310 REM **********************************
00320 OPEN "BOOK.FILE" AS FILE #1
00330 FOR I = 1 TO 6
00340   PRINT #1,B$(I)
00350   PRINT #1,A$(I)
00360 NEXT I
00370 CLOSE #1
00380 REM **********************************
00390 REM ***  PUT FILE DATA INTO PROGRAM   ***
00400 REM **********************************
00410 OPEN "BOOK.FILE" AS FILE #2
00420 FOR I = 1 TO 6
00430   INPUT #2,B$(I)
00440   INPUT #2,A$(I)
00450 NEXT I
00460 CLOSE #2
00470 REM **********************************
00480 REM *** PRINT BOOK COLLECTION REPORT  ***
00490 REM **********************************
00500 PRINT
00510 PRINT
00520 PRINT TAB(15);"BOOK COLLECTION"
00530 PRINT
00540 PRINT "BOOK TITLE";TAB(35);"AUTHOR"
00550 FOR I = 1 TO 6
00560   PRINT B$(I);TAB(35);A$(I)
00570 NEXT I
00580 REM **********************************
00590 REM ***      THE DATA STATEMENTS      ***
00600 REM **********************************
00610 DATA THINK AND GROW RICH,NAPOLEON HILL
00620 DATA COMPUTERS AND DATA PROCESSING,STEVE MANDELL
00630 DATA ECONOMICS,PAUL SAMUELSON
00640 DATA INFORMATION PROCESSING,MARILYN BOHL
00650 DATA THE SNOWS OF KILIMANJARO,ERNEST HEMINGWAY
00660 DATA COST AND MANAGERIAL ACCOUNTING,RONALD HARTLEY
00999 END
```

RUNNH

BOOK COLLECTION

BOOK TITLE	AUTHOR
COMPUTERS AND DATA PROCESSING	STEVE MANDELL
COST AND MANAGERIAL ACCOUNTING	RONALD HARTLEY
ECONOMICS	PAUL SAMUELSON
INFORMATION PROCESSING	MARILYN BOHL
THE SNOWS OF KILIMANJARO	ERNEST HEMINGWAY
THINK AND GROW RICH	NAPOLEON HILL

PSEUDOCODE

```
Start
Dimension the arrays
Start loop, do six times
   Read book title and author
End loop
Start loop, do until flag is not equal to one
   Initialize flag to zero
   Start loop, do five times
      If B$(I) > B$(I + 1)
         Then
            Switch B$(I) and B$(I + 1)
            Switch A$(I) and A$(I + 1)
            Assign one to flag
      End if
   End loop
End loop
Open the book file
Start loop, do six times
   Enter book title from the file
   Enter author from the file
End loop
Close the book file
Print the report headings
Start loop, do six times
   Print book title and author
End loop
Stop
```

MICROCOMPUTERS	
Apple	See Section X of text
Apple Macintosh	See Section X of text
IBM/Microsoft	See Section X of text
PET Commodore 64	See Section X of text
TRS-80	See Section X of text

†